The Autism Toolbox

An Autism Resource for Scottish Schools

Support for Learning Division
Schools Directorate
Scottish Government

Scottish Autism Service Network
and
National Centre for Autism Studies
University of Strathclyde

Aline-Wendy Dunlop, Charlene Tait, Alison Leask,
Lisa Glashan, Anna Robinson and Helen Marwick,
with support from Maggie Smith, Gwen Carr and Tommy MacKay.

ISBN: 978-0-7559-8022-2

The Scottish Government
St Andrew's House
Edinburgh
EH1 3DG

Produced for the Scottish Government by RR Donnelley B57583 03/09

Published by the Scottish Government, March 2009

Further copies are available from
Blackwell's Bookshop
53 South Bridge
Edinburgh
EH1 1YS

The text pages of this document are printed on recycled paper and are 100% recyclable

The Autism Toolbox

An Autism Resource for Scottish Schools

Foreword

Almost every school in Scotland will have at least one child with an autism spectrum disorder because autism occurs in one in 150 children. Autism is a remarkably complex disorder that can be confusing for teachers, parents and support staff. The Autism Toolbox includes up-to-date information from research and practical experience that is easy to understand and apply in the classroom, playground and home. It is essential reading for teachers who have a child with an autism spectrum disorder in their class. I know that the explanations, strategies and resources will become their first source of practical knowledge in schools in all parts of Scotland. Education Authorities will also use the information to plan services to facilitate the successful inclusion and education of children with autism. Undoubtedly The Autism Toolbox will significantly improve the school experiences of such children and will be a model for other countries throughout the world. If this is your personal copy of The Autism Toolbox, ensure you keep it in a safe place as many of your colleagues will want to borrow it.

Professor Tony Attwood
Visiting Professor
National Centre for Autism Studies
University of Strathclyde

Acknowledgements

The Autism Toolbox was commissioned by the Support for Learning Division of the Schools Directorate, Scottish Government, as an outcome of the work of the Autistic Spectrum Disorder Education Working Group which was convened following the publication of the HM Inspectorate Report into Autism and the National Autistic Society's '*make school make sense*' campaign report.

The multi-professional writing team was led by Professor Aline-Wendy Dunlop, Director of the National Centre for Autism Studies, University of Strathclyde. The writing team included Charlene Tait (lecturer) and Lisa Glashan (teacher), who researched and wrote most of the section on Support for Pre-schools, Primary Schools and Secondary Schools; Alison Leask (Chair, Autism Argyll and Autism Consultant with the Scottish Autism Service Network) who wrote the Support for Parents section and led on the Resources section; Anna Robinson (Scottish Society for Autism) who wrote the section on Working with Other Agencies, and Dr Helen Marwick (lecturer) who wrote the Overview of Interventions in section 5.

We extend thanks to:

- Maggie Smith (Development Officer – Inclusion, Learning and Teaching Scotland), who has shared case study material on Autism Spectrum Disorders with us. We have shaped short vignettes based on this material to include in the Toolbox: the full case studies will be published on the LTScotland website
- Participating schools
- Chris Toon, for Annex 3 on behalf of Moray Council
- Fife Council for Annex 2
- Dr Tommy MacKay (Visiting Professor, National Centre for Autism Studies) for his careful reading of the Toolbox and feedback to the team
- James O'Donnelly, South Lanarkshire Council
- Gwen Carr (Occupational Therapist) for her work on sensory issues
- Tom Malone, for the design and layout of the toolbox, and Léonie Docherty for poster design
- The Scottish Autism Network Team whose research is reflected in the Toolbox, and in particular Andy Soares (Web Developer) for his cover and section designs and Lindsey Watson for her secretarial support
- All who gave feedback on drafts of The Autism Toolbox – we have incorporated your advice wherever possible.

Autistic Spectrum Disorder Education Working Group

Liz Hunter (Chair)	Director, Schools Directorate, Scottish Government
Anna Boni	Inspector, Her Majesty's Inspectorate of Education
Carolyn Brown	Fife Council Psychological Service, Fife Council
Laura-Ann Currie	Inspector, Her Majesty's Inspectorate of Education
Joanna Daly	Policy and Parliamentary Officer, National Autistic Society Scotland
Aline-Wendy Dunlop	Chair of Childhood and Primary Studies and Lead Director, National Centre for Autism Studies, Strathclyde University
Carol Evans	Director, National Autistic Society Scotland
Bette Francis	Adult Care and Support Division, Scottish Government
Mike Gibson	Deputy Director, Support for Learning Division, Scottish Government
Stella MacDonald	Consultant and Service User
Robin McKendrick	Head of Branch, Support for Learning Division, Scottish Government
Moira Park	Depute Head Teacher, Carlibar Primary School, East Renfrewshire Council
Shona Pinkerton	Principal, Daldorch School, National Autistic Society Scotland
Veronica Rankin	National Officer, Educational Institute of Scotland
Martyn Rouse	Chair of Social and Educational Inclusion and Director of Inclusive Practice Project, University of Aberdeen
Janet Stirling	Head Teacher, New Struan School, Scottish Society for Autism
Jim Taylor	Director of Education and Support Services, Scottish Society for Autism
Martin Vallely	Professional Services Manager, Children and Families, The City of Edinburgh Council

Authors' Note

Throughout this document we refer to 'Autism Spectrum Disorders' (ASD) to signify children and young people with diagnoses of autism, high functioning autism and Asperger's Syndrome or other autistic conditions as described in DSM IV (American Psychiatric Association, 1994 and 2000) and ICD 10 (World Health Organization, 1992) - to date the two most commonly used diagnostic criteria. We recognise that schools will sometimes work with pupils 'as if' they are on the autism spectrum - perhaps when a process of assessment and diagnosis is underway, or when behaviours strongly suggest that such approaches will be helpful to the individual concerned. Numbers of pupils with ASD attending mainstream education will have a diagnosis of Asperger's Syndrome (AS).

The Autism Toolbox – An Autism Resource for Scottish Schools

Contents

Foreword		i
Acknowledgements		iii
Autistic Spectrum Disorder Education Working Group		v
Authors' Note		vii
Contents		ix
The Autism Toolbox – Overview of Approach		1
	Part 1 - The Policy and Legislative Context	9
Part 1.1	The Policy Context	10
Part 1.2	A Concordat between Scottish Government and Local Government	12
Part 1.3	The Policy and Legislative Context	14
Part 1.4	Strategic Planning for Future Service Provision	16
Part 1.5	Reports on ASD	18
	Part 2 - The Toolbox – Autism in Practice	25
Section 1 - Knowing about Autism		29
1.1	Understanding Pupils on the Autism Spectrum – Defining ASD	29
1.2	Understanding the Autism Spectrum – Prevalence	30
1.3	Diagnosis and Working with ASD	31
1.4	Understanding Pupils on the Autism Spectrum – The Triad of Impairment	31
Section 2 - Guidance and Support for Pre-Schools, Primary Schools and Secondary Schools		39
2.1	Autism Spectrum Disorder – A Highly Individual Context	42
2.2	Strengths and Challenges	44
2.3	Teaching and Learning	48
2.4	Assessment	62
2.5	Individualised Educational Programmes	74
2.6	Classroom Organisation and Classroom Strategies	80
2.7	Differentiation – Principles and Practicalities	92

2.8	The Social Curriculum	100
2.9	Transitions	124
2.10	Whole School Approaches	146

Section 3 – Support for Parents and Families 157

3.1	Working with Parents	157
3.2	Schools' Guidance to Parents – a Reciprocal Relationship?	159
3.3	Communicating Effectively with Parents	161
3.4	Meetings with Parents	164
3.5	Inclusion of Parents of Children and Young People with ASD in the Life of the School	166
3.6	Working with Groups of Parents	168
3.7	What Parents may be doing at Home	171
3.8	Issues for Siblings	173

Section 4 – Working with Other Agencies 179

4.1	What is Multi-agency Working?	179
4.2	Who takes the Lead?	182
4.3	Transitions and Multi-agency Working	182
4.4	Multi-agency Systems	182
4.5	Co-ordinated Support Plans	184
4.6	Top Ten Points for Positive Practice in Multi-agency Working	185
4.7	Multi-agency Involvement – Professional Roles	186

Toolbox References 192

The Autism Toolbox Part 3 – The CD Rom

Part 3 of The Autism Toolbox is contained on the accompanying CD Rom together with the following materials.
(Parts 1, 2 and 3 are also available in electronic PDF format on The Scottish Government website)

Section 5 – Overview of Interventions

5.1 Aims, Areas and Scope of Interventions

5.2 Evidence of Effectiveness of Interventions from a Research Perspective

5.3 Interventions and Educational Settings

5.4 Parental Programmes

5.5 Interventions and Approaches to Supporting Cognitive and Perceptual Styles

5.6 Alternative and Augmentative Communication (AAC)

5.7 Promoting Interpersonal Engagement and Shared Communicative Experiences

5.8 Teaching Social Communication Skills and Social Understanding

5.9 Applied Behavioural Analysis (ABA)

5.10 Cognitive Behaviour Therapy

5.11 Social Stories

5.12 Sensory and Motor Interventions

5.13 Biomedical Interventions

Section 6 – Resources

Section 7 – Building on the Legislative Context – Local Authority Guidance towards Strategic Planning Approaches for Future Service Provision

7.1 The Policy and Legislative Context

7.2 Strategic Planning Approaches

7.3 The Right Training

Section 8 – Directory – Finding Information and Advice

Section 9 – Practice Grids and Posters

Set 1 - Practice Grids (A full set of the Practice Grids can be found in Part 2, Section 2).

Set 2 - Posters

The Autism Toolbox – Overview of Approach

The Autism Toolbox for Scottish Schools is designed to support Education Authorities in the delivery of services and planning for children and young people with Autism Spectrum Disorders (ASD) in Scotland, and will sit alongside existing Local Authority resources. It complements the guidance issued on *Health and Social Care Services for People with Autism Spectrum Disorders.* The intention is to provide a resource to support the inclusion of children and young people with autism spectrum disorder in mainstream education services. The Autism Toolbox is presented in three parts with nine sections overall. Part 1 and Part 2 form the printed version of The Autism Toolbox and are intended to support daily practice. Part 3 is presented on CD Rom.

The guidance is offered in eight main sections. Part 2 Sections 2, 3 and 4 are intended to support daily practice and are grouped together to form 'The Toolbox – Autism in Practice'. None of the material will provide ready answers as autism is a complex condition, but each will support practitioners who seek to tailor their work to enable those with ASD to participate as fully as possible in the daily life of their school.

The Autism Toolbox can be accessed from the Scottish Government Website and from the Scottish Autism Service Network website.

In considering the content of this guidance the Autism Spectrum Disorder Education Working Group (the Working Group) took account of all the recommendations of both the Her Majesty's Inspectorate of Education (HMIE) *Education for Pupils with Autism Spectrum Disorder* (HMIE, 2006a) and the National Autistic Society's (NAS) '*make school make sense'* (Batten and Daly, 2006) reports and have based this guidance on what it considers to be the key issues that build upon the foundations provided by both reports.

This guidance recognises, as was reflected in both reports, that good practice does exist, and highlights a few examples to alert others of the systems and approaches used within current provision.

However, although there is much being done, both reports identify that the capacity exists for developments in a number of aspects in respect of Scottish wide practice. This point is endorsed by the Working Group and has guided its thinking in developing guidelines that will have relevance to all providers, regardless of their current provision.

What follows is what the Working Group considers to be the main issues to be addressed in considering the provision and information available on ASD, particularly in the context of education and closely related fields such as Social Services and Health.

Whether education authorities already have guidance and provide supportive material to schools or these have yet to be fully developed, they should take care to ensure that school staff is aware of the guidance and the provisions that are supplied to support access to the curriculum. A brief overview of the guidance follows -

Part 1 - The Policy and Legislative Context

The first part of The Autism Toolbox for Local Authorities and schools summarises the policy context in Scotland as it affects educational provision, the legislative context in which provision for pupils with ASD in Scotland should be considered and highlights the need for strategic planning for ASD by Local Authorities and their strategic partners. This information is elaborated upon in Section 7 of The Autism Toolbox to be found on the accompanying CD Rom. Part 1 also presents the key recommendations of two reports published in 2006: the HMIE Report into *Education for Pupils with Autism Spectrum Disorder* (Her Majesty's Inspectorate of Education, 2006a) and the NAS *'make school make sense'* campaign report (Batten and Daly, 2006).

Part 2 - The Toolbox - Autism in Practice

The second part of the resource, The Toolbox – Autism in Practice, provides direct advice for day-to-day practice: the guidance in each section is presented in the form of grids which address the impact of autism on key aspects of practice, and relate these to 'How Good is Our School' (HMIE, 2007a) and 'Child at the Centre' (HMIE, 2007b). A file containing the grids is available on the CD Rom.

Section 1 - Knowing about Autism

In order to include and support individual children and young people with autism in mainstream services it is important to have an understanding about the nature of this lifelong, complex spectrum which has day-to-day implications for work in schools. This section emphasises the importance of starting with the person and combining individual understanding with knowledge about autism. It presents an introductory understanding which will help practitioners to feel informed.

Section 2 - Support for Pre-schools, Primary Schools and Secondary Schools

Ten key aspects of practice are addressed in this section, they include:

2.1 Autism - A Highly Individual Context

2.2 Strengths and Challenges

2.3 The Impact of ASD on Teaching and Learning

2.4 Assessment

2.5 Individualised Educational Programmes

2.6 Classroom Organisation and Classroom Strategies

2.7 Differentiation - Principles and Practicalities

2.8 The Social Curriculum

2.9 Transitions

2.10 Whole School Approaches

Examples of practice gathered from field practitioners at all stages of education are threaded through these sections.

Section 3 - Support for Parents and Families

Written by representative parents with long experience of working collaboratively with schools, this section addresses:

3.1 Working with Parents

3.2 Schools' Guidance to Parents - a Reciprocal Relationship?

3.3 Communicating Effectively with Parents

3.4 Meetings with Parents

3.5 Inclusion of Parents of Children and Young People with ASD in the Life of the School

3.6 Working with Groups of Parents

3.7 What Parents may be doing at Home

3.8 Issues for Siblings

Section 4 - Working with Other Agencies

This section offers a brief guide to working with the range of professionals who may be involved with children and young people with autism and their families. The complexity of autism may determine that a range of professionals are involved:

4.1 What is Multi-agency Working?

4.2 Who takes the Lead?

4.3 Transitions and Multi-agency Working

4.4 Multi-agency Systems

4.5 Co-ordinated Support Plans (CSPs)

4.6 Top Ten Points for Positive Practice in Multi-agency Working

4.7 Multi-agency Involvement - Professional Roles

Part 3 - CD Rom of Printable pdf Files

Part 3, containing Sections 5-9, is produced on the enclosed CD Rom, and not in the printed resources. It is available through the Scottish Government website and the Scottish Autism Service Network website. With millions of 'hits' every time the word 'autism' is keyed into the web (at the time of publication this was 18,500,000) a filter is needed to identify useful and reliable information. The resource section is intended to provide reliable information, useful links, and to illustrate resources that may be helpful in practice and are readily available at the time of going to press.

Section 5 - Overview of Interventions

This section offers an overview of interventions and draws on the research literature to describe their effectiveness, strengths and possible drawbacks. It is included in the Toolbox as practitioners working with children and young people with autism are likely to draw from these interventions in their own practice, and need to be able to discuss their key strengths with parents and families.

Section 6 - Resources

In this section we have included some key texts, web links and references. Print based material is shown by book or report cover, with a brief description and a note of how to access the resource. There are 100 sources listed here and these are referenced where appropriate throughout the document.

Section 7 - Building on the Policy and Legislative Context - Local Authority Guidance Towards Strategic Planning Approaches for Future Service Provision

This section considers the Scottish legislative and policy context in more detail, expands on the brief outline of legislation provided in Part 1 and suggests guidance for Local Authorities on strategic planning approaches.

Section 8 - Directory - Finding Information and Advice

Information about where to get help from knowledgeable others is important in the dissemination of good practice. Key organisations and local contacts are included here. Information is correct at the time of going to press, however such information is quickly outdated, and so readers are advised to check on the Scottish Autism Services Network for routes to up-to-date information.

Section 9 - Practice Grids and Posters pdf Files

It is recognised that Toolbox users may wish to print off some of the material included in Part 2 – the practice grids are available here in pdf format. There is also a set of 8 posters related to sections of the Toolbox which may be ordered in full A1 size from the National Centre for Autism Studies.

Set 1 - Practice Grids

Set 2 - Posters

1. A Resource for Scottish Schools - The Autism Toolbox
2. Guidance for Schools
3. Support for Parents and Families
4. Sharing Responsibility - Working with Other Agencies
5. Early Interventions
6. Pupils' Involvement in all matters which affect them
7. The Policy and Legislative Framework
8. Highlighting Resources - Finding help and information

The Autism Toolbox

Part 1

The Policy and Legislative Context

Part 1 – The Policy and Legislative Context

Education Authorities, schools and early years settings have a major role to play in supporting the Scottish Government's 5 strategic objectives by expanding opportunities, increasing access to education, as well as increasing the opportunities available to, and the achievements of, pupils and young children on the autistic spectrum. This part of The Autism Toolbox summarises the policy context in Scotland as it affects educational provision, the legislative context in which provision for pupils with ASD in Scotland should be considered, and highlights the need for strategic planning for ASD by Local Authorities and their strategic partners. Each aspect is expanded in Section 7 of The Autism Toolbox (to be found on the enclosed CD Rom). This part also presents the key recommendations of two reports published in 2006: the Her Majesty's Inspectorate of Education (HMIE) Report into *Education for Pupils with Autism Spectrum Disorder* and the National Autistic Society (NAS) Scotland's '*make school make sense*' campaign report.

Part 1.1 The Policy Context

This Toolbox should be regarded as being a contribution towards the achievement of the Scottish Government's five strategic objectives, which are:

- **A wealthier and fairer Scotland**

  To be achieved by enabling businesses and people to increase their wealth and more people to share fairly in that wealth.

- **A healthier Scotland**

  To be pursued by helping people to sustain and improve their health, especially in disadvantaged communities, and by ensuring better, local and faster access to health care.

- **A safer and stronger Scotland**

  Delivered by helping communities to flourish, becoming stronger, safer places to live, through offering improved opportunity for a better quality of life.

- **A smarter Scotland**

  Achieved by expanding opportunities for Scots to succeed, from nurture through to lifelong learning, ensuring higher and more widely shared achievements.

- **A greener Scotland**

  Seeing improvements in Scotland's natural and built environment and the sustainable use and enjoyment of it by all.

It should be noted that these objectives apply equally across all policy portfolios within the remit of the Scottish Government. In taking forward the smarter objective, and within this context, the Scottish Government are guided by the following six principles:

- By investing in effective services for all children to ensure every child gets off to the best start in life.
- Having an international perspective to promote an understanding of Scotland and our place in the world and challenging our ambitions against the achievements of other countries.
- Having high aspirations and challenging all to aim high.
- Being egalitarian and embracing the Scottish tradition of the democratic intellect as part of our approach to learning ensuring education and learning are at the heart of the community, supporting communities and promoting community self-reliance, as well as promoting the safeguarding of our environment and natural resources.
- Focusing on the child and the learner, providing support and learning journeys that respond to individuals' needs and potential.

Further and in implementing these principles the Cabinet Secretary for Education and Lifelong Learning has stated that the Scottish Government's education policies will focus on:

- Early intervention
- Supporting vulnerable children and their families
- Improving the learning experience in school
- Developing skills and lifelong learning
- Promoting innovation in higher education

These polices are supported by the introduction of *A Curriculum for Excellence* that seeks to enable all to become:

- Successful learners
- Confident individuals
- Effective contributors
- Responsible citizens

Part 1.2 A Concordat Between Scottish Government and Local Government

"This concordat sets out the terms of a new relationship between the Scottish Government and local government, based on mutual respect and partnership. It underpins the funding to be provided to local government over the period 2008-09 to 2010-11.

The new relationship is represented by a package of measures. It is endorsed by both the Scottish Ministers and by the COSLA Presidential Team."

Scottish Government (2007a, p.1)

Scottish Government's strategic objectives as outlined in Section 1.1 will be realised through the Concordat signed by representatives of Scottish Government and of COSLA on 14th November 2007. The publication of the Concordat coincided with the publication of *The National Performance Framework* (Scottish Government, 2007b) which sets out the strategic objectives and the national outcomes that the Scottish Government expects to see from its investment. These outcomes are measured by 45 national indicators and targets.

The Concordat is recognised by signatories to be "both ambitious and ground breaking" (p.7). Its intention is to shift the relationship between Scottish Government and local government in such a way as to avoid micro-management at central Government level and to free local authorities and their partners to deliver on agreed over-arching outcomes. The various components of the package are included in the Concordat Agreement. As part of the new responsibilities of local authorities there is greater flexibility and decision making at a local level, and a clear requirement to be answerable in terms of achievement of the agreed outcomes. Policy developments will be jointly negotiated between Scottish Government and local government, through COSLA. Some such areas of interest have already been identified such as the development of an early years/early intervention strategy, and provision of support for kinship carers. Such policy developments are inclusive and will therefore have an impact on children and young people with ASD and their families as well as the wider population in all aspects of local authority responsibility:

- Education - including compulsory school education, adult and community education
- Social work - including community care
- Community leadership and community planning
- Addressing poverty and promoting social cohesion
- Roads and transportation
- Planning and the environment
- Police and fire services

- Economic development
- Housing
- Leisure and library services
- Cultural services

The *Early Years Framework* (Scottish Government, 2008a), has been jointly developed by the Scottish Government and COSLA as part of their Concordat agreement and was launched in December 2008. The *Early Years Framework* relates to national outcome target number 5 'Our children have the best start in life and are ready to succeed', it is also a policy initiative which forms one of the six guiding principles of the Scottish Government's Smarter objective. In developing a strategic approach to early intervention, Ministers and COSLA have identified some key principles – these are elaborated further in Section 7 of The Autism Toolbox.

Part 1.3 The Policy and Legislative Context

A number of key Acts and priorities come together to influence the inclusive environment of Scottish education: a very brief overview is given here: more detail may be found in Section 7 on the CD Rom and on the poster ' Policy and Legislative Context' also on the CD Rom.

Key legislation includes:

1.3.1 The Standards in Scotland's Schools etc Act 2000 (also 7.1.1)

The Act includes a presumption in favour of providing mainstream education for all children. However the context in which this should be implemented is one that specifically allows for education to be provided elsewhere, this is because it will always be necessary to tailor provision to the needs of the individual child, and to make available a range of mainstream and specialist provision, including special schools, to meet the needs of all pupils.

1.3.2 The Education (Additional Support for Learning)(Scotland) Act 2004 (also 7.1.2)

The 2004 Act replaced the system for assessment and recording of children and young people with special educational needs, and introduced a framework for identifying and addressing the additional support needs of children and young people who face a barrier to learning. It places duties on education authorities and requires other bodies and organisations to help education authorities to meet their duties.

1.3.3 Disability Discrimination Act 1995 (DDA) (as amended by the Special Educational Needs and Disability Act 2001) (also 7.1.3)

The amended 1995 Act makes it unlawful for education providers to discriminate against disabled pupils and prospective pupils in the provision of education and associated services in schools, and in respect of admissions and exclusions.

1.3.4 Education (Disability Strategies and Pupils' Educational Records) (Scotland) Act 2002 (also 7.1.4)

There is a requirement for responsible bodies to prepare and implement accessibility strategies to improve over time access to education for pupils and prospective pupils with disabilities. There is also a requirement that, if requested to do so, responsible bodies must make a copy of the accessibility strategy available to any person. New guidance is in preparation.

1.3.5 Disability Discrimination (Public Authorities) (Statutory Duties) (Scotland) Regulations 2005 (also 7.1.5)

These regulations reflect the fact that the Disability Discrimination Act 1995 is amended by the Disability Discrimination Act 2005: the 2005 Regulations provide a specific duty on educational authorities to produce a disability equality scheme to help them fulfil their general duty: The Disability Equality Duty (DED).

1.3.6 The Disability Equality Duty (DED) 2006 (also 7.1.6)

The Disability Equality Duty – the general duty is introduced in the amended Disability Discrimination Act 1995. There is a requirement for any public body to develop and implement a Disability Equality Scheme (DES) for the whole authority and a separate education DES to cover their function as an education authority.

1.3.7 Getting it Right for Every Child (GIRFEC) (also 7.1.7)

Getting it right for every child is a key priority for the Scottish Government as it contributes to its strategic objectives. The Government is committed to policies which help Scotland's children and young people fulfil their potential. *Getting it right for every child* is a national programme that is changing the way adults and organisations think and act to help **all** children, young people and their families grow, develop and reach their full potential.

1.3.8 A Curriculum for Excellence (also 7.1.8)

A Curriculum for Excellence provides explicit statements of the aims of education in Scotland, concepts which have long been implicit. In summary, the purposes of education are to enable all young people to become: successful learners; confident individuals; responsible citizens and effective contributors.

The development of these capacities, attributes and capabilities lies at the heart of work on curriculum renewal.

1.3.9 The Early Years Framework (also 7.1.9)

The *Early Years Framework*, at its simplest, is about giving all our children the best start in life and identifying the steps the Scottish Government, local partners and practitioners in early years services need to take to make a start on that journey. At the heart of this framework is an approach which recognises the right of all young children to high quality relationships, environments and services which offer a holistic approach to meeting their needs.

Part 1.4 Strategic Planning for Future Service Provision

In Scotland, education authorities have a duty to ensure that they provide adequate and efficient educational provision for any child or young person with additional support needs and this of course includes children and young people with ASD. In ensuring that these needs are met, education authorities must also make a wide range of provision available and ensure that the teaching methods used in schools meets the needs of each individual pupil. This provision may be made in specialist units or bases within mainstream schools, or by outreach, or peripatetic support teams. Provision may also be provided in Special Schools.

This guidance is designed to support education authorities in the delivery of these duties and as a first step considers the legislative and policy context in which these duties exist.

Local authorities' Strategic Planning for Future Service Provision will include definition of strategy or direction for ASD, and making decisions on allocation of resources to pursue this. Strategic Planning should take account of the policy and legislative context summarised in Part 1, the advice offered in Parts 2 and 3 of The Autism Toolbox, and the more detailed Legislative section in Section 7, and should be predicated on the recognition that ASD is a lifelong condition. Services will need to offer at least some level of support throughout life. This highlights the importance of strategic analysis, direction and action planning in the light of the need for joined up services, consultation with families and service users, training of staff and the right services for ASD.

A number of key elements in strategic planning are listed here and elaborated in Section 7 which can be found on the CD Rom included with The Autism Toolbox.

Key elements in strategic planning:

- Statistics: Local authorities' provision and information collation
- A varied range of provision and publication
- Social and education inclusion
- Information to Parents
- The Right Training

Additionally, these annexes provide helpful information:

Table 1 – Annexes to Section 7 (CD Rom)

Annex 1	Specific planning duties
Annex 2	Collecting data on ASD – exemplar from Fife Council's ASD Data Survey
Annex 3a	Proforma for Pupils with an Autism Spectrum Disorder – exemplar from Moray Council
Annex 3b	Whole school organisation and training for managing pupils with autism spectrum disorders – exemplar from Moray Council
Annex 4a	Present training and development opportunities for ASD in Scotland
Annex 4b	Scottish National Training Framework – *The Development of a National Training Framework for Autistic Spectrum Disorders, A Study of Training for Professionals Working in the Field of ASD in Scotland (MacKay and Dunlop, 2004*)
Annex 5	Information to Parents

Part 1.5 Reports on ASD

Two significant reports into ASD were published in 2006: *Education for Pupils with Autism Spectrum Disorders (*HMIE, 2006a) and the NAS *'make school make sense' campaign report* (Batten and Daly, 2006). Both reports were considered by the Autism Spectrum Disorder Education Working Group.

1.5.1 HMIE's 'Education for Pupils with Autism Spectrum Disorders' Report

A focused inspection of Education for Pupils with Autism Spectrum Disorders was reported in 2006 by HM Inspectorate of Education. In the foreword by HM Senior Chief Inspector Graham Donaldson, stated that:

"Autism spectrum disorders, as the name suggests, do not represent a single nor straightforward set of needs to be met. The challenges facing education and other professionals, and the young people whose needs are being addressed, are considerable. The key is to see past the presenting issues, often behavioural in nature, to the communication disorders beyond that and to find what works for each individual concerned. This report is about the extent to which the needs of pupils with autism spectrum disorders are being met across a range of educational establishments and services. It evaluates the progress pupils make in their learning and the extent to which they achieve to their fullest potential within the various forms of provision.

*Education for Pupils with Autism Spectrum Disorders (*HMIE, 2006a) highlights the variety of provision and arrangements for meeting the needs of pupils with ASD. Across the various forms of provision, the task group found that most pupils were making good progress towards the targets in their individualised educational programmes. However, these programmes were frequently deficient in either the attention given to addressing the underlying ASD needs or conversely in addressing achievement across the curriculum. Also, in many cases, the progress of pupils was not tracked systematically, with the result that schools and authorities did not have sufficiently detailed information about the achievement of pupils with ASD. In addition, parents were not always kept fully informed about the range of provision available for their children. Training for all staff involved in the education of pupils with ASD was also a key area for development. We need to do better in these highlighted aspects. It is important to get them right because if things go wrong, they can have serious consequences." (p.iii).

The *Education for Pupils with Autism Spectrum Disorders* report (HMIE, 2006a) made eight key recommendations: these follow.

Recommendation 1:

Education authorities should ensure that they hold complete information on the numbers of pupils with autism spectrum disorders for whose education they are responsible to ensure that they develop a coherent strategy for meeting a range of needs. This information should include details of provision for these pupils. Allocation of support and resources should not be restricted to those pupils with medical diagnosis of autism spectrum disorders.

Recommendation 2:

Education authorities should ensure that they have a suitably varied range of provision to meet the wide and varying needs of pupils with autism spectrum disorders. They should publish details of their provision for autism spectrum disorders, including planned future developments.

Recommendation 3:

Education authorities should ensure that schools prepare clear and effective individualised educational programmes for all pupils with autism spectrum disorders and use them as planning tools to meet the specific and broader learning needs of individual pupils. They should ensure that schools also use individualised educational programmes to track pupils' progress towards meeting their potential. The Scottish Executive, education authorities and other agencies should work together to coordinate support for pupils with autism spectrum disorder, where there is a need. Education authorities should work with health boards to develop clear procedures for early identification of children with autism spectrum disorders.

Recommendation 4:

Schools should ensure that pupils with autism spectrum disorders are given appropriate opportunities to gain an understanding of the social world they live in and to develop life skills which they can use outside school. Pupils should be given full opportunities to identify and develop their personal strengths.

Recommendation 5:

Schools should ensure that they maximise opportunities for pupils with autism spectrum disorders to be included socially and educationally with mainstream peers.

Recommendation 6:

Education authorities should ensure that parents receive full information about the provision they make for autism spectrum disorders. They should also ensure that parents are informed of the options available to them when their child transfers from stage to stage or school to school. Education authorities and schools should work closely with parents of children with autism spectrum disorders to plan for progression, particularly at times of transition. They should involve parents in relevant training events about autism spectrum disorders. Where appropriate, people with autism spectrum disorders could be invited to contribute to training programmes for parents and staff.

Recommendation 7:

Education authorities should ensure that teaching and support staff have access to a programme of staff development relating to autism spectrum disorders. Continuing professional development at an appropriate level should be available to all staff in schools where there are pupils with autism spectrum disorders. Specialised training should be provided for teachers and non-teaching staff working directly with pupils with autism spectrum disorders. The Scottish Executive should work with training providers to ensure that a comprehensive and progressive programme is available.

Recommendation 8:

Education authorities and agencies should work together to develop plans, share strategies and commit resources to ensure that pupils with autism spectrum disorders receive appropriate support in line with their needs. Plans should be regularly evaluated and reviewed and openly shared with parents.

1.5.2 NAS '*make school make sense*' Campaign Report

The National Autistic Society makes a special focus each year on a topic of importance to people with ASD, their families and carers. In 2006 their campaign focused on the school experiences of children and young people. Reports based on membership surveys were published in England, Wales, Scotland and Northern Ireland. The Autism Spectrum Disorder Education Working Group considered the key points raised in the Scottish '*make school make sense*' report (Batten and Daly, NAS, 2006). A parental survey informed the report which highlighted that "significant failures in our education system are causing misery for many of the 46,000 families affected by autism in Scotland": in the perception of the parents surveyed these failures include that:

- Over a third of children with autism have been bullied at school (pp.18 and 22).
- Over a third of families had to wait longer than a year before their child received any support at school (p.19).
- 1 in 110 children has autism but there is currently no requirement for teachers to undertake any training in autism and just one in three parents are satisfied with the level of understanding of autism at their child's school (p.25).

'make school make sense' campaign report
(Batten and Daly, 2006)

The NAS report highlights that the survey was undertaken at a time when the new legislation of the *Education (Additional Support for Learning) (Scotland) Act 2004 (ASL Act)* (Scottish Executive, 2004a) would not yet have had an impact as the ASL Act came into force from November 2005. Three 'demands' were made as an outcome of this report and were considered in detail by the Education Working Group, these are:

- The right school for every child.
- The right training for every teacher.
- The right approach in every school.

These concepts presented in the Scottish version of the *'make school make sense'* report which contains recommendations for both the Scottish Government and local authorities, are fully elaborated on pages 23 and 24 of that report and in Section 7 (CD Rom).

The Autism Toolbox

Part 2

The Toolbox – Autism in Practice

Part 2

The Toolbox

Autism in Practice

The Toolbox provides direct advice for day-to-day practice: the guidance in each section is presented in the form of grids which address the impact of autism on key aspects of practice, and relate these to 'How Good is Our School' (HMIE, 2007a) and 'Child at the Centre' (HMIE, 2007b).

Section 1 - Knowing About Autism

In order to include and support individual children and young people with autism in mainstream services it is important to have an understanding about the nature of this lifelong, complex spectrum which has day-to-day implications for work in schools. This section emphasises the importance of starting with the person and combining individual understanding with knowledge about autism. It presents an introductory understanding which will help practitioners to feel both informed and more skilled.

Section 2 - Support for Pre-Schools, Primary Schools and Secondary Schools

Ten key aspects of practice are addressed in this section.

Section 3 - Support for Parents and Families

Working together with parents and families in the eight main ways highlighted in this section will ensure appropriate links with families.

Section 4 - Working with Other Agencies

No single professional group can meet the needs of pupils with autism in isolation from other services. Seven elements of multi-agency working are covered in this section.

The Autism Toolbox

Part 2
Section 1

Knowing about Autism

Section 1 - Knowing about Autism

1.1 Understanding Pupils on the Autism Spectrum - Defining ASD

The first step to understanding pupils on the autism spectrum is to have an awareness of the terminology used and to know what such terms may indicate in terms of educational, social and emotional needs. It is essential to build a relationship with and to develop personal knowledge of the individual child or young person, in this way it is possible to begin to appreciate that autism spectrum disorder (ASD) is part of the story of who the child is as a person with a unique profile that includes their personality, strengths, challenges, likes and dislikes. A significant number of individuals with a diagnosis of autism also have learning disabilities (Vermeulen, 2001). ASD is considered to be a neuro-developmental disorder (Trevarthen, 2000) with the impact on development occurring before 3 years of age (World Health Organisation, 1992), however recent insights into autism suggest that the impact of the neuro-developmental differences in autism takes place from 8-14 months (Trevarthen and Aitken, 2001).

Terms and their meaning

Autism

Autism is commonly typified by what is known as the triad of impairments (Wing 1996). These are:

- Social Communication
- Social Interaction
- Social Imagination and Flexible Thinking

High Functioning Autism (HFA)

This term is often used but is not found in the diagnostic criteria. It was used to describe people whose Social Communication, Social Interaction and Social Imagination is affected by autism, but whose IQ is within the normal range (as with Aperger's Syndrome (AS) – no clinical impairment and a standard score of over 70 IQ), before the term Asperger's Syndrome (AS) came into common usage in the 1990s. Debates continue as to whether HFA and AS are interchangeable terms.

Asperger's Syndrome

Asperger's Syndrome is typified by:

- Severe and sustained impairment in social interaction
- Restricted, repetitive patterns of behaviour, interests and activities
- Significant impairment in social, occupational or other aspects of functioning

Individuals will have had no clinically significant delay in language development. It is however important to note that there may be significant issues with the understanding, processing and use of social language. Individuals with Asperger's Syndrome have no clinically significant cognitive impairment. Consequently their cognitive abilities fall within the normal range (American Psychiatric Association, 1994). As with HFA the disabilities associated with autism will have an impact on learning and schooling. Children with a diagnosis of Asperger's Syndrome may also be noticeably clumsy.

Atypical Autism

This term is used to describe children where the onset of differences in development has occurred after 3 years of age and/or where insufficient differences are noted in one or two of the areas of impairment needed for a diagnosis of autism. Atypical autism is a diagnosis that is usually associated with profound cognitive impairment (World Health Organization, 1992).

Other linked conditions

There are other conditions that are considered by some to be part of the wider Autism Spectrum such as Rett's Syndrome and Childhood Disintegrative Disorder. However, some commentators feel that, in time, as diagnostic criteria are reviewed such conditions may no longer be viewed as part of the broader spectrum (Ozonoff, Rogers and Hendren, 2003).

Autism as a Context

It should also be noted that ASD overlaps with other conditions: most commonly this includes Epilepsy and Attention Deficit Hyperactivity Disorder (ADHD) and Obsessive Compulsive Disorder (OCD). Each of these conditions occur independently of autism, but many people with ASD also present with other conditions – thus autism can be a context for a range of difficulties. This adds to the complexity of meeting each person's needs appropriately.

1.2 Understanding the Autism Spectrum - Prevalence

Autism Spectrum Disorder (ASD) is the term used to describe a range of conditions that impact on the development, learning, processing and perception of individuals. It is a lifelong condition that has been thought to affect 60 per 10,000 children (PHIS, 2001). Numbers of epidemiological studies continue to be published, e.g. Fombonne (2005) and aim to clarify prevalence figures. More recently a number of studies suggest that ASD is more common than previously thought, for example the Washington, USA Centers for Disease Control and Prevention (CDC) released, through its Morbidity and Mortality Weekly Report (MMWR) on 8th February 2007 that the prevalence of autism in six research sites was 1 in 150. This report states, "Findings from this first U.S. multi-site collaborative study to monitor ASD prevalence demonstrated consistency across the majority of sites..... Average

ASD prevalence across all six sites was 6.7 per 1,000 children aged 8 years". Whilst they state this is not a nationally representative sample, nevertheless they make the point that "These results indicate that ASDs are more common than was believed previously." This view is supported by the work of Baird, Simonoff, Pickles et al, (2006) who also found the prevalence of autism and related ASDs to be far greater than recognised previously. The abstract of their study makes the point that "Whether the increase is due to better ascertainment, broadening diagnostic criteria, or increased incidence is unclear. Services in health, education, and social care will need to recognise the needs of children with some form of ASD, who constitute 1% of the child population."

Both the National Autistic Society and the Office of National Statistics suggest that a rate of around 1 in 100 is currently the best estimate of the prevalence in children. This would mean that there are around 6,900 pupils with ASD in Scotland. More detail of Scottish statistics is given in Section 7 on the CD Rom.

1.3 Diagnosis and Working With ASD

The recognition that a person has an Autistic Spectrum Disorder can occur throughout the lifespan and typically diagnosis of Asperger's Syndrome is more subtle and often occurs later than for those who have a more classic presentation. This means that there will be children and young people whose ASD goes undiagnosed, if not unrecognised during schooling. If a parent or colleague expresses a concern, or if you are working with pupils whose behaviour leads you to think they may be on the spectrum, it is important to seek appropriate advice. It is not always appropriate or necessary for a person to have a formal diagnosis, but sometimes diagnosis ensures appropriate services. Educational Psychologists can be a helpful source of advice and are often members of diagnostic teams. As with all disability it is essential that schools work closely together with families and seek further professional guidance to help with concerns raised.

1.4 Understanding Pupils on the Autism Spectrum – The Triad of Impairment

It is important to acknowledge that an increasing number of individuals on the spectrum, their families and the professionals involved in their care, support and education are beginning to question and indeed reject the term 'impairment' in favour of thinking about 'differences'. That said Wing's Triad (1996) can be a helpful starting place in trying to map out how ASD may be impacting on thinking, learning and social development and interaction, by 'unpacking' the Triad.

The various aspects of the triad are not distinct and all will impact on each other. Despite common challenges associated with the triad there is no such individual as the typical person on the spectrum/ with autism. Educators will benefit from having as broad an understanding of the potential impact on social communication, social interaction and social imagination and flexible thinking as possible. It is essential to be aware that impact may at times be extremely subtle. It is tempting to view behaviour, responses and mind sets through the lens of typical development. However knowing a pupil has ASD provides a context for understanding from an entirely different perspective. 'Looking normal' can sometimes work against such understanding and leave these children and young people very vulnerable.

In unpacking the Triad, highlights of some of the behaviour associated with each aspect are presented. This is by no means exhaustive, and current research presents a more complex view of autism, but is intended to help with recognition of the spectrum of impact on individuals. Observable communication differences in pupils with ASD are outlined below.

Social Communication

The drive to communicate in social situations is challenging for many people with ASD. Across the spectrum people may vary from being non-verbal to talking at others without being aware of picking up on typical responses. In these situations a person's expressive language may not be matched by appropriate receptive communication skills. Look out for these behaviours:

- May have no spoken language or be non-verbal.
- May have limited understanding and use of non-verbal language such as social gestures, pointing, responding to and following requests.
- May have limited language that is used in a functional way e.g. may be able to make requests to meet basic needs.
- Social language is limited and this is likely to compound issues related to social interaction. Emotional vocabulary may be limited or absent, and facial expressions may be 'flat'. This can give the false impression that persons with ASD lack feelings and emotions. It is therefore vital that the emotional health and well being of children and young people across the autism spectrum is considered.
- May echo speech. The term for this is **echolalia.** Some individuals will echo speech as a way of helping them to process information and to make sense of what is said. There may be other reasons for echolalia such as anxiety. It is therefore important to observe the level and use by the child of this feature of language.
- Pronoun reversal. This simple action means that an individual may say, "You want a drink" when they mean "I want a drink".
- There may be idiosyncrasies in the way individuals with spoken language talk. Such differences can include speaking in a monotonous tone. There may also be difficulties with the rhythm, pitch and intonation of speech. Many children on the spectrum speak with an accent that differs from their local accent; this is usually an American accent.

- Literal interpretation of language is a common feature in children with ASD. Metaphors and similes can be difficult to interpret. Difficulties in abstracting intention and implied meaning can lead to many social misunderstandings.
- As a result of a tendency to take language literally, pupils with ASD may be unable to understand the subtleties of classroom behaviour and may speak up to report on other pupils' behaviour when their peers might maintain a steady silence – this too can lead to isolation in the peer group.
- Understanding facial expressions. Subtle expressions may be difficult to perceive and process. Children may also find it problematic to join the communicative dots: meaning they may not make the connections between what is said, how it is said and the body language and facial expressions that are used in congruence. This can lead to misunderstandings as some will not find it easy to interpret others intonation to derive the correct meaning.
- Individuals with ASD may have an unusual way of using social eye gaze. Eye gaze is a helpful social communicative tool that typically developing individuals may use to include or exclude people from conversation. It can also signal that conversations are about to end or that there is something in our field of reference that we wish to draw to another's attention. Children and young people with ASD may avoid eye contact or use it very intensely and as a result will stare at people in a way that can be unnerving. Some people with ASD have reported that they use their peripheral vision as they find eye contact or the more usual use of eye gaze uncomfortable. Others say they don't make eye contact as it distracts them from hearing and understanding what is being said.
- A diagnosis of Asperger's Syndrome is given when there is no significant language delay and no cognitive impairment. There is also the presence of intense and restricted special interests often referred to as obsessions. The verbal and non verbal social communication difficulties of children with Asperger's Syndrome may be more subtle. They may have very fluent speech but have a very narrow range of topics of conversation. Their style and use of language may be quite formal or precocious. They are likely to use the same style of communication regardless of the context. Therefore unlike typically developing children they may not differentiate between the language used with friends in the playground and language used in the classroom. The tendency to more formalised pedantic language can often set them aside from their peers. Restricted interests and obsessions can limit their ability to access social situations and to develop reciprocal relationships as their one-sided, narrow view can be off- putting to others.
- Children and young people with ASD frequently behave in ways that are difficult for others to understand. Such behaviour may be a form of communication. It can be more productive to view behaviour in this way and to develop supportive communication strategies rather than to assume there is a behaviour problem *per se*.

Social Interaction

Social interaction is often considered to be at the core of ASD. The innate drive for social contact that most individuals have is fraught with complexity when a child is on the spectrum. There are a huge range of issues that relate to social interaction across the spectrum. The following is indicative of some of the observable social behaviour of pupils on the spectrum:

- Some children may appear to have no desire for social contact and may appear to be socially aloof. Such children tend to have a more classical presentation of autism.
- Conversely children with Asperger's Syndrome may have a strong desire for social contact but will struggle in a number of the following areas.
- Appreciating the reciprocal nature of interaction can be challenging. Such children may find it difficult to engage in shared activities, team games and social conversation.
- A lack of social curiosity can inhibit the development of relationships. Not knowing how to build and use social knowledge of other people, their likes, dislikes, interests, ambitions etc can be a barrier to friendship.
- Pupils with ASD have a tendency to be rule bound. This can be a tremendous asset in terms of compliance within the classroom but can greatly inhibit social development. In social situations the rules are more fluid and flexible and often change depending on contextual and environmental factors. Such adjustment and flexibility is challenging and stressful for pupils with ASD.
- Children and young people may have a very superficial, literal understanding of friendship e.g. a friend is someone you sit next to in class. The complex incremental development of relationships is often hidden to the child on the spectrum and consequently social misunderstandings are frequent, stressful and demoralising.
- Pupils with ASD may appear to show little or no awareness of the needs and feelings of others. This can often be interpreted as a lack of empathy. It is however more likely that what is lacking is understanding. Individuals with ASD often have to solve relationship puzzles by intellect rather than intuition. This can lead to misunderstandings and also indicates support is needed to acquire the skills to problem solve in social situations.
- Social imitation is a key skill in developing social behaviour. Whilst many children with ASD are excellent mimics they find social imitation more challenging. Pupils with ASD are less likely to observe and follow the social behaviour of other pupils. They may therefore appear to lack motivation to conform to the behavioural norms of the classroom but it is more likely they lack the knowledge of what is expected and that they are not gleaning such information from observation of their peers.
- There is a great risk of vulnerability for pupils with ASD particularly those with Asperger's Syndrome. Such children often have an awareness of their differences and a desire for

"normality". This can render them vulnerable to bullying and manipulation by other children who may capitalise on their social naivety in the classroom and the playground as well as on the way to and from school.

Social Imagination and Flexible Thinking

Imagination supports a great deal of our social and intellectual growth. It has an obvious role in early life in relation to play, social and cognitive development. There are often noticeable idiosyncrasies in terms of the nature and quality of play observed in very young children with ASD e.g. they may focus on aspects of a toy such as the wheels of a toy car and enjoy them on a sensory level rather than as a typically developing child might. Socially, a child with autism may be observed to play alongside other children rather than with them, again the implications are significant. Social imagination plays a critical role in guiding social behaviour. Individuals with ASD find it very difficult to think in a future-oriented way and to speculate about what may occur and how they might react, behave or respond to a given situation. Consequently their social behaviour is often reactive. Individually, children and young people may be limited in their capacity to rehearse mentally how they might behave at assembly, on a school outing, to a supply teacher or to a whole range of scenarios about which typically developing children may be able to make assumptions because they can assemble a coherent cognitive picture.

Other issues include:

- Appreciating the perspective of others and recognising the impact one's own behaviour can have on other people.
- The retention and application of sequences may be difficult to keep in mind. Visual reminders may be needed to support the execution of routines, even those that are regularly repeated.
- Many pupils with ASD will prefer to complete tasks rather than return to them as breaking and shifting attention can be difficult. There are supports that can be put in place to compensate for this but it may be a source of anxiety.
- Generalising skills and behaviour may be problematic.
- Pupils with ASD are prone to rigid and inflexible thinking and this can manifest in a whole range of ways e.g. insistence on sameness: the pupil may always want to sit in the same place. Such rigidity can impinge on other areas such as diet; many children with ASD eat a limited range of foods.
- Literal interpretation of language linked with inflexible thinking can lead to a range of issues e.g. conceptualising the passage of time. If the pupil is told "we will finish at 10am" he/she is likely to expect to finish precisely at that time. Similarly vague references to time such as "we will do that later" may provoke anxiety as they are meaningless to the child with ASD.

Children and young people with ASD tend towards routine and sameness indeed for some there is a high level of dependency on both. This aspect of ASD is often misconstrued as meaning that there must never be any change around pupils with ASD. This is misleading. Change and unpredictability are part of daily life. However the pupil will not become de-sensitised to change just because it occurs around them and it can be a source of stress and anxiety. It is important to recognise the extent to which this may be an issue for an individual pupil. Minimising unnecessary change and involving the pupil where possible will be beneficial.

The key to thinking about these issues is to have an awareness of Social Communication, Social Interaction, and Social Imagination and Flexible Thinking and to understand the different impact of each aspect of the Triad for each individual pupil.

The Autism Toolbox

Part 2
Section 2

Guidance and Support for Pre-Schools, Primary Schools and Secondary Schools

Section 2

Guidance and Support for Pre-Schools, Primary Schools and Secondary Schools

The Standards in Scotland's Schools etc Act (2000) heralded the presumption of mainstreaming for all children. This means that it is now more likely than ever that local authorities, schools and individual teachers will be involved in the education of children and young people who are on the autism spectrum. The impact of autism on development and learning is pervasive and complex: it can be challenging to accumulate a body of knowledge that is sufficient in relation to the range of needs and challenges that are experienced on an individual level.

Any individual or body concerned with providing an education that will meet the needs of pupils on the autism spectrum adequately will require information and guidance. In this section a number of key aspects of provision for autism are highlighted. It is however important to establish from the outset that whilst the guidance given will be essential to effective inclusion, teaching and learning of pupils on the spectrum it is also likely to be beneficial to all pupils, and to developing and sustaining a more inclusive ethos across the school as a whole.

The guidance given covers a number of key areas:

2.1 Autism Spectrum Disorder - A Highly Individual Context

2.2 Strengths and Challenges

2.3 The Impact of ASD on Teaching and Learning

2.4 Assessment

2.5 Individualised Educational Programmes

2.6 Classroom Organisation and Strategies

2.7 Differentiation - Principles and Practicalities

2.8 The Social Curriculum

2.9 Transitions

2.10 Whole School Approaches

The aim is to enable already skilled and competent teachers to integrate and use ASD specific guidance in parallel with their skills in teaching, understanding and supporting children, young people and their families. Where relevant, reference has been made to current educational and ASD specific documents and reports such as, *How Good is our School: The Journey to Excellence Part 3* (HMIE, 2007a), *The Child at the Centre* (HMIE, 2007), *Education for Pupils with Autism Spectrum Disorder*

(HMIE, 2006a), *A Curriculum for Excellence: Building the Curriculum 3* (The Scottish Government 2008b) and *Assessment is for Learning* (Learning and Teaching Scotland, SQA, Scottish Executive, 2006). Where quality indicators are referred to these apply across all stages, and take account of the strong connection between *Child at the Centre* and *How Good is our School*.

There are no prescriptive solutions. This guidance is intended to support authorities and school staff to develop innovative, individualised and creative approaches to teaching pupils with ASD. The aim is to raise attainment and minimise potential difficulties by being proactive. Booth and Ainscow (2002) suggest that inclusive schools are those where policy, practice and culture promote both the presence and active participation of all pupils. When the needs of pupils on the spectrum are well recognised, understood and supported such outcomes are possible. Additionally the needs of other pupils will also be met.

The Autism Toolbox

Part 2

Section 2.1

Autism Spectrum Disorder – A Highly Individual Context

2.1 Autism Spectrum Disorder – A Highly Individual Context

The current terminology of ASD is rooted in impairment. In such a context it can be easy to overlook the talents, strengths and competencies of individuals. It is therefore essential to consider ASD in a way that takes account of assets as well as challenges.

For each pupil there will be a highly individual profile that emerges and that will have implications for learning.

Anxiety is likely to be an issue to a greater or lesser extent for all children with ASD. The impact of anxiety on learning and coping cannot be underestimated. The manifestation of anxiety will vary in individuals and may result in a range of behaviours such as repetitive behaviours, running off, withdrawal, aggression or other concerning behaviours. Everyday activities that many pupils will take in their stride may trigger feelings of stress and anxiety in pupils on the autism spectrum. Consequently there is no ready made solution for supporting and teaching pupils on the autism spectrum. It is therefore important for teachers to develop an appreciation of the potential impact of ASD on learning and behaviour and to integrate this with their skills as educators in order to meet what can often be highly individual needs.

Pupils on the spectrum are likely to have encountered significant challenges in accessing the social world. Self esteem and self confidence will have been dented and fractured on many occasions, consequently many children and young people with ASD experience poor self image and poor self esteem. Repeated social and educational difficulties can serve to reinforce such experiences and can have an impact on motivation and well-being. Pupils with ASD need appropriate expectations placed upon them and will need specific and individualised support and clear directions (Lamarine, 2001) to attain goals and to achieve in school.

Knowing where to look and how to recognise strengths in the profile of pupils on the spectrum can be beneficial. Vermeulen (2001) suggests it is useful to understand both the attributes of individuals on the spectrum and the challenges that they may face. The role of the effective teacher is to capitalise on these skills to the benefit of the pupil.

The Autism Toolbox

Part 2

Section 2.2

Strengths and Challenges

2.2 Strengths and Challenges

2.2.1 Meeting the Rights of People with ASD in Education

The rights of all pupils in Scotland are respected under the UN Convention of the Rights of the Child (Scottish Government, 2007c). In 1996 the European Parliament adopted the Autism Charter as a written declaration of the rights of people with ASD. Existing guidance for schools emphasises the right of all pupils to be consulted on matters which affect them. Whilst the status of the Charter of Rights for People with Autism remains adopted as a written statement, rather than enacted, there are particular items in the Charter that provide a helpful guide for schools, for example:

- The right of people with autism to lead independent and full lives to the limit of their potential.
- The right of people with autism to an accessible, unbiased and accurate clinical diagnosis and assessment.
- The right of people with autism to accessible and appropriate education.
- The right of people with autism (and their representatives) to be involved in all decisions affecting their future; the wishes of the individual must be, as far as possible, ascertained and respected.
- The right of people with autism to the equipment, assistance and support services necessary to live a fully productive life with dignity and independence.
- The right of access of people with autism (and their representatives) to all information contained in their personal, medical, psychological, psychiatric and educational records.

From the written declaration adopted by European Parliament 1996

The "Education, (Additional Support for Learning) (Scotland) Act 2004 strengthens the rights of children with additional support needs and their parents to have their needs identified and addressed effectively and for children to have their views taken into account in that process and in discussing, monitoring and evaluating their learning" (Scottish Government, 2007c). Meeting rights means recognising diversity by taking account of the nature of ASD and in particular acknowledging the need for reasonable adjustments to enable the participation of children and young people with ASD in education.

2.2.2 Strengths and Challenges

Vermeulen (2001) offers an interesting comparison between typical thinkers and those with ASD citing a range of strengths in "autistic thinking". Strong points include analytical thinking, an eye for detail and a tendency to be logical. In some contexts these aspects may be viewed as disadvantageous however with the support of empathic and creative teaching such skills can be used to promote achievement. It can be very helpful to view the impact of ASD in this way. By beginning to identify differences in thinking and processing teachers can be more responsive and creative in terms of differentiating approaches and resources to increase accessibility to the curriculum for learners on the spectrum. Vermeulen illustrates that the range of strengths in thinking can lead to original, artistic and creative outcomes. This is clearly reflected in the variety of artwork and literature people on the spectrum generate.

It is therefore important to move beyond a view that the characteristics of individuals on the spectrum always result in challenge and or impairment. This does not mean that the needs of individuals should be overlooked but that there should be equal emphasis on the identification of skills, talents and abilities regardless of how diverse they may be or how difficult they are to identify.

Curriculum for Excellence (Scottish Government, 2008b, p.17) advocates "All children and young people should experience personalisation and choice within their curriculum, including identifying and planning for opportunities for personal achievement in a range of different contexts. This implies taking an interest in learners as individuals, with their own talents and interests." Scottish school pupils have a right to be consulted on all matters which affect them.

Example 1 - Pupil involvement in all matters which affect them

A primary pupil demonstrated a strong fear of going to the doctor. This had a huge impact on both himself and his family, as trips to the doctor were extremely stressful and avoided whenever possible.

Through discussion with his parents and school staff it was agreed that the Early Childhood Practitioner (ECP) would work with the pupil to devise a programme which aimed to reduce his level of anxiety in these situations.

The pupil was fully involved in planning out the small steps in this programme and the ECP worked closely with the GP practice. Activities in the programme included role play, sharing stories about the doctor, playing with real objects, social stories, trips to the surgery, talking to the receptionist, making appointments, talking to the GP, and finally, attending an appointment. After two weeks of daily activities the pupil was happily visiting the GP surgery and continues to do so one year on.

It is recognised that this can be testing for staff who may feel they have insufficient insight into ASD to be able to make an accurate judgement. However drawing on and applying advice from the "Assessment" section of the toolbox will increase confidence and encourage staff to engage with pupils in a way that allows their abilities as well as needs and rights to be recognised.

The Autism Toolbox

Part 2
Section 2.3

Teaching and Learning

2.3 Teaching and Learning

All topics in this section relate to the impact ASD has on the various aspects of teaching and learning. An overview of how processing information, cognition and motivation for learning are affected is essential in order to set all the following issues in context.

There are three principal explanations of autism: Affective explanations of autism, cognitive explanations of autism and explanations which combine both affective and cognitive perspectives.

Many individuals with ASD cope with sensory processing difficulties and these can have an impact on day-to-day functioning.

Additionally, as highlighted in the 'Knowing about Autism' section, Wing's 'Triad of Impairments' (Wing and Gould, 1979) provides insight into a range of observable behaviours associated with ASD. In an educational context it is essential to marry this with an understanding of both affective and cognitive explanations of autism in order that behaviours and approaches to learning are understood and supported by appropriate teaching methods.

The motivation of individuals with autism is also an important area to consider.

2.3.1 Affective Explanations of Autism

Affective explanations of autism focus on differences within the systems of emotional and interpersonal connection which are fundamental to personal relatedness and motivations to engage and communicate with others (Kanner, 1943; Hobson, 1993; Trevarthen, Aitken, Papoudi and Robarts, 1998). Differences in these systems are understood to impact on shared feelings, shared play, and joint attention, and influence social and communicative development and the development of self-concept. These systems underpin many subtle, almost hidden, aspects of communication and interaction, such as the timing of social interactions, sympathetic awareness of the feelings of another person, and awareness of a shared focus of attention. Implications of this may be seen in difficulties in holding conversations, such as turn-taking and keeping on topic, difficulties in the awareness of listener reaction and the emotional responses of others in activities, and difficulties in playing with others and forming friendships.

2.3.2 Cognitive Explanations of Autism

Currently 3 dominant psychological theories prevail and attempt to provide explanations of autism, these are that:

- Individuals on the spectrum have an impaired Theory of Mind mechanism
- Individuals on the spectrum have a weak drive for Central Coherence

- Individuals on the spectrum have impairments in a range of executive functions

Theory of Mind

Theory of Mind emerges in typical development around 2 – 4 years. It is the cognitive mechanism that enables the ability to appreciate the perspectives of others and to recognise that others have thoughts, desires, beliefs and mental states that are unique. Significant research in relation to deficits in theory of mind in children with ASD was conducted by Baron-Cohen, Leslie and Frith (Frith, 1989). Whilst poorly developed theory of mind does not provide a complete account of the spectrum and associated challenges, it can be helpful in unpacking some of the aspects of social behaviour that are perplexing for children on the spectrum and difficult for those around them to understand. An impaired theory of mind may be implicated in a range of the behaviours observed in children and young people on the spectrum such as the difficulties and challenges they face in:

- Empathising
- Appreciating the perspective of others
- Forming and sustaining relationships
- Social prediction
- Social curiosity
- Interpreting the intentions of others
- Predicting and understanding the consequences and the impact of behaviour on others

(Adapted from Cumine, Leach and Stevenson, 1998)

Central Coherence

Central Coherence is the simultaneous cognitive processing of a range of information or stimuli that may appear unrelated to build meaning and understanding. This process enables us to make sense of contextual information and is implicated in a range of cognitive skills as well as guiding behaviour. It is suggested that in individuals with ASD the drive for central coherence is weak. This may result in fragmented processing of details and information that makes it difficult for individuals to construct meaning. This may result in serial processing i.e. one thing at a time rather than simultaneous processing (Frith, 1989). The implications of weak processing in this area may explain why it is difficult for individuals on the spectrum to:

- See and make connections in a range of contexts
- Generalise skills – seeing the relationship between what is expected and what is already known

- Focus attention
- Appreciate alternative perspectives
- Cope with environmental variables or that which is unknown or unfamiliar
- Choose and prioritise
- Organise and plan

(Adapted from Cumine et al, 1998)

Example 2 - Idiosyncratic focus of attention

A teacher was working with a primary one class. Anne, a pupil with ASD, was particularly difficult to engage in teacher led activities or settle to tasks. It was story time and the pupils were gathered on the carpet. Anne seemed to be listening very intently to the story and the teacher was delighted. At the end of the story Anne put up her hand, the teacher was very excited because this was the most engaged Anne had been. When the teacher asked Anne what her question was Anne stated, "Your nostrils are different shapes!"

Executive Dysfunction

Executive function difficulties are not unique to individuals with ASD however research suggests that for this population they are more severe and are different in type and onset than in other conditions (Klin, Volkmar and Sparrow, 2000) This is perhaps one of the most complex areas as executive function is the term used to describe a collection of cognitive mechanisms that are implicated in a range of areas such as:

- Behaviour that is involved in developing and working towards a goal
- Systematic problem solving
- Flexibility of thought and behaviour
- Controlling inappropriate impulses and self-control
- The guiding of behaviour by mental models or internal representations

(Jordan, 1999)

Whilst no theory completely explains the spectrum there are elements of all that are helpful in guiding educationalists towards appropriate supports and teaching strategies based on an appreciation of the diverse cognitive styles of children and young people on the spectrum. Theories can therefore be used to inform practice and to develop empathy for individuals on the spectrum.

2.3.3 A Combined Theory of Autism

Recent explanations of autism suggest that it is helpful to combine understandings from cognitive and affective theories of autism, using insights from both neuropsychological and developmental models (Sigman, Spence and Wang, 2006). Affective theories are based on developmental knowledge and developmental approaches, rather than heavily relationship based interventions, and may provide a way forward in the early years. By linking insight into early social difficulties with cognitive explanations more suited to older children, it is possible to see an important link between the capacity to respond through joint attention and the better adult outcomes associated with the acquisition of spoken language by age five.

2.3.4 Sensory Processing

Many individuals on the spectrum report difficulties with processing sensory information. This remains a relatively under researched area and therefore understanding is by no means advanced in this area. Theorists and researchers continue to debate and investigate the possible cause of sensory integration and processing difficulties for people across the autism spectrum however at a practice level, accepting and supporting are perhaps more essential to understanding the impact on teaching and learning. Given the frequency with which such issues are raised by and on behalf of individuals with ASD, this aspect of the spectrum is specifically addressed in sections 2.3.8 and 2.3.9.

2.3.5 Motivation

Children and young people on the spectrum are capable of prolonged periods of engagement and focused attention. This is generally evident when the focus is related to something that is in keeping with their special interest or that they find motivating. Children and young people may also present as lacking in attention or display behaviour that is distracting for other pupils.

Young children are likely to need repetitive and specific teaching in order for them to acquire appropriate learning behaviour such as sitting, sharing, turn taking, listening, asking and responding to questions. They may find collaborative or group learning challenging and may appear not to have the same natural curiosity as their peers. In order to acquire learning behaviour and to enable pupils on the spectrum to sustain motivation and engagement it will be important to establish what is motivating for them and to maximise the use of intrinsic and extrinsic personal motivators in their teaching and learning. It is important to recognise that these may be non traditional and linked to specific interests. Social motivators such as supporting peers or pleasing the teacher or their parents may not impact to the same degree as it might with typically developing children and young people. Similarly children and young people may, for some of the reasons discussed find it difficult to formulate personal goals and targets and to work strategically towards them. They may not recognise or value their achievements. This is an area where individual and personalised support may be needed. Specific issues relating to motivation are highlighted throughout this section.

Example 3 - Motivation and confidence

Our Primary School Unit decided to enter the annual Determined to Succeed Making Movies Competition sponsored by Glasgow City Council and the Glasgow Film Theatre. This offered a concrete opportunity for the P6/7 children to work collaboratively on a project from beginning to end, to generalise their learning and to celebrate success. The children needed to decide on a storyline and write a synopsis of the film which was the initial entry to the competition. We were one of ten primary schools to be successful and entered into the second stage of the competition. The children were involved in characterisation, developing their storyline within the limits of the synopsis through writing storyboards, acting the parts, using digital video cameras for filming, sound recording and finally editing the work to the required length of time. All of the children contributed to the project and were brimming with confidence and pride when presenting their project, 'Cuckoo Cop', to visiting teachers, parents and peers.

2.3.6 Stress and Anxiety

Pupils on the autism spectrum are known to experience high levels of anxiety which impacts on their ability to function appropriately in some contexts and be receptive to learning. Staff may question the inconsistent patterns and root cause of inappropriate behaviours, e.g. he can do it in the drama group so he should be able to do it in the gym hall. We all perform differently depending on our environment and mood, e.g. an experienced driver can negotiate familiar routes while chatting, listening to music, eating, etc. but if you were to drive in an unfamiliar city these skills would be much poorer, you may only be able to concentrate on direction signs, finding the radio or another person talking distracting.

Stress levels must be monitored and reasonable allowances made to enable pupils to cope with the environment and access the curriculum as fully as possible.

Sometimes the source of a pupil's anxiety will be clear, however, what can be more challenging for adults is when pupils respond adversely to anticipated events or reactions, for example, bells ringing, school outings, responses from peers. These responses and feelings are very real for pupils on the autism spectrum even when they are associated with events or activities usually perceived as enjoyable or innocuous.

Example 4 - Anticipation

Andrew, a Primary 2 pupil was frequently showing signs of distress and would attempt to leave the classroom. Discussion with his parents revealed this was also occurring at home. No clear trigger was apparent to staff or parents. After a period of persistent, close observation it became clear that Andrew had an intense fear of the animated BBC2 jingle. The problem for staff and parents in identifying this trigger was that Andrew was already upset by the time it appeared having anticipated the event.

This was resolved by being able to acknowledge with Andrew that staff knew it upset him and that they would ensure that the TV was turned off before the logo would appear.

2.3.7 The Impact of ASD on Teaching and Learning (Grid 1)

The Impact of ASD on Teaching and Learning	
Impact of ASD	**Responding to the needs of pupils with ASD**
Links to HGIOS Quality Indicators	
1.1 Improvement in performance 1.2 Fulfilment of statutory duties 2.1 Learners' experiences 5.1 The Curriculum 5.2 Teaching for effective learning 5.3 Meeting learning needs 5.4 Assessment for learning 5.5 Expectations and promoting achievement 5.6 Equality and fairness 5.7 Partnership with learners and parents 5.8 Care, welfare and development	8.1 Partnerships with the community, educational establishments, agencies and employers 8.2 Management of finance for learning 8.3 Management and use of resources and space for learning 8.4 Managing information 9.1 Vision, values and aims 9.2 Leadership and direction
Refer to HMIE *Education for Pupils with Autism Spectrum Disorder* Recommendations 3, 4, 5, 7 and 8	

The Impact of ASD on Teaching and Learning	
Impact of ASD	**Responding to the needs of pupils with ASD**
• Difficulty forming and sustaining relationships due to limited awareness and appreciation for the perspective of others. This may be interpreted by others as a lack of empathy.	• An acknowledgment of how significant social interaction skills are in enabling pupils to engage with a range of learning opportunities. • An acceptance that difficulties in this area are a core aspect of ASD and that children will benefit from being valued as individuals with a different social perspective. • Time is needed to explore and identify learning opportunities within social situations. • A range of approaches can be adapted to support learning in this area (See Section 6 - Resources 25, 26, 28, 45). Additionally natural opportunities for social learning need to be maximised e.g. playground activities, dining hall and community activities.

The Impact of ASD on Teaching and Learning	
Impact of ASD	**Responding to the needs of pupils with ASD**
• Predicting and understanding the consequences and the impact of behaviour on others may be problematic.	• Understanding the social behaviour of pupils with ASD can be complex. It is tempting to view the responses and reactions and motivation of pupils from a typical perspective. Whilst behaviour needs to be addressed it is essential that attempts are made to understand the ways in which ASD has been a factor and that behaviour can often result from communication difficulties or from prolonged exposure to highly stressful situations. It is important to remember that some pupils with ASD will find even the most basic of social situations anxiety provoking.
• Seeing and making connections in a range of contexts may be challenging. Skills learned in one environment may not automatically be replicated in another.	• There is a need for continuous assessment across all areas. Assessment will need to take account of environmental and contextual factors. Do not assume because a child demonstrates competence in one setting that this will be generalised to a range of contexts. This means more detailed and comprehensive approaches to assessment may be required to ensure an accurate profile of skills and abilities is being formed.
• Focus of attention may be inconsistent and out of step with teachers' expectations.	• Visual supports may be needed to enable the pupil to direct their attention appropriately e.g. use of maths window, highlighting sections that need to be read. The teacher may also need to check that the focus is as expected as it may frustrate pupils to feel that they are carrying out tasks when they find a mismatch of expectations. Adults may also become frustrated by what may appear to be a lack of concentration and focus. In reality most children with ASD will be trying hard to process information but may not always be on the right track.

The Impact of ASD on Teaching and Learning	
Impact of ASD	**Responding to the needs of pupils with ASD**
• Coping with the unknown or unfamiliar may be stressful and may have a negative impact on behaviour.	• Plan and prepare for new situations by using strategies such as appropriate visual supports, social stories or by a familiar and trusted adult explaining what will happen. This is especially important if plans need to change. Pupils with ASD are less likely to respond negatively to change if it is signalled and explained in a way they can understand.
• Choosing and prioritising may be problematic and may be linked to difficulties with predicting outcomes and consequences.	• Sometimes it may be necessary to limit choices in order to make the decision more manageable for the pupil. This does not need to mean that access to experiences or opportunities are closed off but that pupils with ASD may need to learn the consequences of decision making in a more incremental way.
• Self and task organisation, planning and working sequentially and systematically may be difficult and idiosyncratic.	• Strategies which support planning such as using checklists, schedules or colour coded work sheets will support problems with prioritising and working in a systematic way.
• Flexibility of thought and behaviour: The ability to cope with change and interpret and act on information in a range of different contexts can be problematic. This may result in a tendency for rigid thinking and processing that manifests in inflexible behaviour patterns and responses.	• It is important that such inflexibility is not misinterpreted as belligerent or non compliant behaviour. Staff need to understand the child's perspective and support them to work through the inflexibility. Pupils will need help to understand that people have different thoughts and feelings to their own. Pupils need to consider alternative responses to challenging situations in a supportive non-judgemental environment.

The Impact of ASD on Teaching and Learning	
Impact of ASD	**Responding to the needs of pupils with ASD**
• Controlling inappropriate impulses and self-control. Pupils may be compelled to engage in a range of behaviours that may be considered impulsive or repetitive. E.g. flicking light switches on and off.	• It is important to establish: • Is the behaviour a problem? • If so who is it a problem for? • What purpose or function does the behaviour serve? • Why might a pupil respond in this way? • What steps can be taken to support them to behave differently? • What can you offer to compensate or motivate the child in place of the behaviour? • These are key questions because adults need to be aware that pupils with ASD will present a wide range of challenges, it is impossible to tackle everything at once, therefore it is important to establish why behaviour may be viewed as problematic. If you simply attempt to extinguish a particular behaviour, an equally or indeed more inappropriate behaviour may develop.
• Reflection on one's own actions, behaviours, experiences and expressions may be limited. This may manifest in an inability to place oneself in an experience or to see the relationship between their actions, outcomes and the responses of others.	• Strategies that promote self awareness and self reflection are important. This can be reinforced by consistent use of pupil self evaluation tools. Consolidation that focuses, not just on content, but on process, e.g. what did you do, who did you do it with, what occurred, how might it have been done differently. This is a core area of difficulty for pupils on the spectrum, they are likely to need ongoing teaching and support to be able to successfully locate themselves in their own experiences and to be able to reflect on those experiences for future learning or habituation of actions.

2.3.8 The Impact of Sensory Issues on Learning

Children with ASD often experience sensory processing issues that may present in an obvious or subtle fashion. The impact of these sensory sensitivities can be significant, and what can be perceived as bad behaviour may in fact be a sensory response to an uncomfortable stimulus. We have 7 different sensory systems and a child may experience processing difficulties in one or more systems:

- Vestibular (movement/balance)
- Proprioceptive (body awareness)
- Tactile (touch)
- Visual (sight)
- Olfactory (smell)
- Auditory (hearing)
- Gustatory (taste)

It is important to allow the child time to 'be autistic' rather than to expect him to comply with normal behavioural patterns at all times. Whilst it is not appropriate, and indeed can be distracting for other pupils, if a child is hand-flapping all the time, it is essential to take account of this and create times when he can indulge in sensory behaviour. It is suggested that the child has a 'sensory box' containing various textured, vibrating or visual toys, that he is able to spend 5 minutes playing with at scheduled times throughout the day. Consultation with an Occupational Therapist may be useful in order to obtain further information on classroom strategies specific to your pupil, and for assistance in creating a sensory box suitable for the individual pupil's needs.

Children who have difficulties with sensory processing can often have issues with co-ordination, so may present as having problems with writing tasks or self care skills such as tying shoelaces, doing zips and buttons, or cleaning themselves effectively after being at the toilet. Again please consult an Occupational Therapist for support to address these issues.

The Impact of Sensory Processing Issues in ASD on Learning Grid provides some general ideas for adapting the school environment to suit the child with ASD. It is by no means exhaustive, and for far more comprehensive suggestions the following resources included in the CD Rom are helpful.

(See Section 6 - Resources 15, 44).

2.3.9 The Impact of Sensory Processing Issues in ASD on Learning (Grid 2)

The Impact of Sensory Processing Issues in ASD on Learning	
This grid highlights some aspects of behaviour that may have a sensory foundation. The suggested strategies will not apply to all children and should not be viewed as a blanket approach. Before implementing it is advisable to at least discuss potential strategies with an Occupational Therapist to ensure appropriateness.	
Tactile Processing Issues	**Responding to the needs of pupils with ASD**
• Child is uncomfortable with light touch and can become upset / aggressive if touched unexpectedly.	• Ensure the child is seated near the back and side of the class so he can see others moving towards him. • Delineate the area the child is to sit on during 'Circle Time' or floor work by using a carpet tile (even better give each child their own tile so as not to make the one child different). Ensure others are not sitting too close. • Ensure the child is either at the front or the back of the line for coming in/out class. Allow the child to be door monitor so he can hold the door open and all others can pass through ahead of him. • Arrange for the child to be allowed into the dinner hall ahead of their peers so he can get sorted and seated before the rush starts. • Forewarn the child before you touch him, by saying his name first and moving through his visual field to reach him. • Do not force the child to participate in messy play e.g. finger painting etc. but allow him alternatives such as using a paintbrush.
Visual Processing Issues	**Responding to the needs of pupils with ASD**
• Child finds bright lights uncomfortable.	• Natural light is a better option than strip lighting, both from a visual and auditory perspective, so avoid artificial light sources if it is a bright day. • Allow the child to wear a skip cap; if not allowed in class then at least allow him to use in the playground and for PE classes being held outside.

The Impact of Sensory Processing Issues in ASD on Learning	
• Child uses vision as a stimulus.	• Keep classroom environment as clutter-free as possible. If your preferred teaching style is to have busy walls then ensure the child has a screened off workstation with high sides, blank walls and a visual timetable only. • Allow the child some small visual toys for their sensory box, that he may play with during timetabled 'sensory breaks'.
Auditory Processing Issues	**Responding to the needs of pupils with ASD**
• The child is easily distracted by loud or extraneous noise.	• Shut doors or windows to reduce external noise. • Pre-warn the child before any tests of the fire alarm system. • Allow the child to use headphones whilst working. • Ear plugs might help in situations such as assembly/ dinner hall etc. During assembly ensure the child is seated at the end of a row, next to the teacher/adult if possible. • Reduce the amount of electrical equipment used during times of concentration. • The noise of a pencil on paper can be uncomfortable and the child may prefer to use a ballpoint pen.
• The child hums constantly (either to block out extraneous noise or because he is seeking auditory input).	• If the child needs to hum to concentrate, teach him to do so quietly. Position him in class where he is less distracting to others. • Giving the child a vibrating toy to hold in this hand whilst working, or allowing him to sit on a vibrating cushion can reduce the degree of humming.
Olfactory Processing Issues	**Responding to the needs of pupils with ASD**
• The child is sensitive to smell.	• Be aware that your perfume or aftershave might elicit an adverse reaction in a child with olfactory sensitivity. • Avoid the use of air fresheners etc in the classroom. • Be aware of the strong smells of some cleaning products.

The Impact of Sensory Processing Issues in ASD on Learning	
Concentration Issues	**Responding to the needs of pupils with ASD**
• The child needs to calm and focus.	• Get the whole class to do 'chair press-ups' prior to any writing activity. • Use weighted 'wheatgerm bags' laid over the child's knees, shoulders or back of the neck to provide additional proprioceptive input during desk based tasks. • Have plenty movement breaks throughout the day.
• The child tends to rock in chair or fidget.	• Allow the child to play with a fidget toy whilst working and listening. Small keyrings or pencil toppers can be a discreet way of providing a 'fidget opportunity'. • Provide the child with a 'Movin'sit' cushion or allow them to sit on a therapy ball during periods when intense concentration is required. • Have plenty movement breaks throughout the day. • Use a 'Movin'sit' or therapy ball as above. • Carry out action songs (e.g. 'Head, Shoulders, Knees and Toes' or 'Alive, Alert, Awake, Enthusiastic') as a class activity prior to periods of concentration.
• The child appears slouched or lethargic.	• Precede any period of sitting with a burst of active movement e.g. star jumps, skipping etc.
Organisational Skills	**Responding to the needs of pupils with ASD**
• Children with ASD benefit from structure and routine.	• Use visual timetables to enable the child to know what comes next. • Use a timer for set pieces of work and for 'sensory breaks'. • Ensure that trays and workbooks are clearly labelled. • For secondary school pupils ensure that workbooks, timetables, school plans and classroom doors are colour coded.

The Autism Toolbox

Part 2

Section 2.4

Assessment

2.4 Assessment

Assessment is a crucial element in meeting the needs of any pupil; however, for pupils on the autism spectrum it is even more important to establish an accurate pupil profile on which to base educational targets. Pupils on the autism spectrum are not a homogenous group; there is no standard educational assessment or approach which can be 'applied'. Even recognised autism specific strategies used indiscriminately, or without consideration of a pupil's individual learning style, impact of their autism, or environmental factors, could be ineffectual or detrimental.

Assessment of pupils with ASD is not achieved through a tick list or prescriptive set of tasks. It is individual to each child and relies on careful observation, identification of concepts or skills which require further exploration, dialogue with parents and other professionals, and reflective interpretation of this information.

Factors that will be important in relation to assessing pupils across the autism spectrum are that:

- Assessment should ideally be carried out in a range of environments. Children may perform well in a given situation but may not transfer or use the skill in another. Such inconsistencies may be attributed to changes and variations in the environment, personnel or resources used. It may be important for the purpose of the assessment task to be clear to the pupil as it may appear meaningless and out of context and may therefore have an impact on motivation to engage.
- Assessment processes may need to be an eclectic mix of information from different sources which can be collated to form a holistic profile. A range of professions may be involved to supplement the knowledge and information gathered by classroom staff. Ongoing collaboration is necessary as the assessment process is not static but will continue to evolve. Cumine et al (1998) offer a valuable observation profile that is helpful when starting to develop a profile.
- Information from home and parental perspectives is vital: Parents have a great deal to contribute to both the informal and formal assessment process. Parents may face quite different challenges to the adults in the education setting. They may be able to offer insight into inconsistencies in performance or competence. It is important to acknowledge that parents are also on a journey of discovery with their children and may not have benefited from good information in order to help them understand their children in terms of the impact of ASD.
- Standard approaches to assessment might not always be viable for children on the spectrum e.g. standardised psychological assessments that are not standardised for an ASD population. There are no curricular areas which will necessarily be problematic for pupils with ASD, and therefore they should in the first instance have the same opportunities

as their peers. However, it is not uncommon for children with ASD to have difficulties with elements of the formal testing process, requiring that some adaptations may have to be made. In some instances pupils may be unable to engage with formal testing and alternatives will need to be sought.

- Standard observation and planning formats tend to be curriculum driven and do not focus on the fundamental areas of difficulty for pupils with ASD. The social curriculum is as important as the formal or academic curriculum, assessment must consider social and communication skills e.g. social interaction, language and communication, play/imagination, independence, self awareness, emotional understanding.
- The developmental profile of children and young people with ASD can be mixed or spiked. They may have strengths and abilities in keeping or indeed beyond their developmental age. In some areas, conversely, skills may be far below their developmental age/stage in other areas. The pupil may be very inconsistent in the execution of tasks. They may demonstrate competency but then appear to have lost the skill or the motivation to carry out the task therefore ASD is central and not peripheral.
- Assessment will inform key areas for inclusion in educational target setting and future planning. Targets should not be solely academically driven. A balance between functional self help, life skills and academic achievement will be necessary in order to meet needs arising from ASD as well as supporting academic attainment.
- Assessment should also incorporate and value wider achievements. Such achievements may be non traditional, however it is important to acknowledge and develop success or ability in a range of areas. Wider achievements should be recognised in order to boost and maintain self esteem of pupils. Children and young people with ASD often do not see themselves reflected in the usual celebrations of achievement in schools.

Example 5 - Wider achievement

A mainstream secondary school develop a two year Duke of Edinburgh Award pilot project aimed specifically at those children who would ordinarily shun the challenges that such an endeavour entails. The course was adapted so that difficulties associated with the autism spectrum (e.g. poor spatial awareness, proprioception and motor planning) could be anticipated, planned-for and overcome allowing pupils to gain recognition for their achievements. With the support of senior management, the programme was embedded into the curriculum and offered as an option to designated pupils at the end of S2 with the first awards gained two years later.

Children with ASD are often reluctant to participate in activities that make demands of them in areas in which they have a relative weakness and these can therefore become barriers to learning and personal development.

continued overleaf

The Duke of Edinburgh's Award encourages all pupils to develop:

- Increased self-confidence and self-esteem
- The skills needed to become part of a team
- A consideration for others
- Understanding of countryside and conservation
- Greater awareness of benefits of healthy eating
- Improved fitness
- Increased friendship with peers
- Broader personal links with wider community
- Lots of fun times
- Memories for life

For the Award to be meaningful, it was important that 'success' had to be earned and this also meant that 'failure' had to be present for the challenge to exist. An important part of the learning process was in helping pupils to see occasional setbacks as learning opportunities and in supporting them to develop resilient mindsets when facing tasks that they did not initially consider to be achievable.

The Supported Award would prepare pupils for the world of independent living, further education and work and thus equip them with the real skills that life would inevitably demand.

The award programme was delivered through three 55 minute lessons per week over two years.

Pupils completed all sections of the Award but each was adapted according to the individual needs of children with ASD, many of whom had difficulties with:

- Balance, coordination and movement (co-morbid dyspraxia)
- Sensory sensitivities (hypo and hyper sensitivities)
- Dysexecutive Syndrome (planning, organising, memory, self-management)
- Spatial awareness

The parents of children who have participated in the supported programme have spoken of the child's:

- Increased independence
- Heightened skill levels
- Enthusiasm for outdoor activities
- Improvements in willingness and ability to work with others
- Greater resilience and determination to overcome adversity

(Interview)

2.4.1 Example 6 - Completed pupil profile

The following example shows one approach to recording a pupil profile. A blank copy of the template below is available as Exemplar 1 - Pupil Profile Template, which can be found in the CD Rom included with the Toolbox in the 'Autism Exemplars' folder.

Primary School

Supported Placements

Pupil Profile

Name: Jimmy
Date of birth: 25/02/01
Primary Stage: P2
Reported by: Mrs G
Present at meeting: Mrs P, Mrs G, Mr and Mrs T
Date: 18/08/05

Report approved by:
Home:
School:
Additional Agencies:

Personal and Social Development

Interaction, Social Awareness and Play
Peers Jimmy prefers to mix with younger children or to play alone with his dinosaurs. He enjoys playing shops, making comics or playing games where he is the organiser or in charge of things.
Adults Jimmy relates well to familiar adults and enjoys talking to and interacting with them – especially when they are willing to engage in his interests. He has a good relationship with Tom, who enjoys playing rough and tumble games with him.

continued overleaf

Home
Jimmy enjoys family life. He has a close relationship with his family members and enjoys talking about and sharing his experiences with his teachers and peers at school.
General (Social Awareness)
Jimmy seems aware of his place in society most of the time and will alter his behaviour in different social situations but only to a certain degree. Sometimes he seems unsure as to how to behave and will display inappropriate behaviour. Jimmy is aware of dangers in society and in the environment, although his parents are still concerned that he would forget rules of safety if something of interest caught his eye. It is possible that Jimmy would forget road safety rules or wander off if he were to be distracted.

Body Awareness, Movement and Self-help Skills
General (Body Awareness/Movement)
Jimmy's movements can, on occasion, appear quite clumsy. He can sometimes find it difficult catching and batting a ball. His gross motor skills are improving and he is happy to climb trees although he is wary of large open spaces and heights. Jimmy's fine motor skills are also developing. There is an improvement in his writing as he attempts to leave spaces between words and when using left handed scissors his cutting skills are good. When Jimmy draws things that are of interest to him he likes to pay attention to detail. Jimmy is aware of the parts of his body and will respond to feelings of hunger and thirst. Jimmy has a high pain threshold. This is obvious as he has to tolerate his eczema which can become very itchy, inflamed and bleed. Jimmy does not like to see blood and will ask for a plaster if his eczema causes bleeding in school.
Home (Self-help skills) *Independence skills* Jimmy is happy to make a good attempt at doing things for himself. Although he prefers to have a bath than a shower, he will shower if it is for a particular reason such as before or after going swimming. *Toileting* Jimmy will not use the toilet outwith home. He has had severe constipation, requiring medication from the doctor and will panic if he has to use an unfamiliar toilet without his mum. *Dressing* Jimmy is able to dress himself, but sometimes chooses not to. He is very particular about textures and cannot tolerate a shirt and tie, he has become used to wearing a polo shirt but is always unhappy if he has to wear a new one for the first couple of weeks. *continued*

Sleeping

Sleeping is a problem for Jimmy. He is reluctant to settle himself at night and relies on Mum to rub his back throughout the evening until he falls asleep. This process can go on for quite a while. Jimmy usually settles fairly late.

Eating

Jimmy eats a lot but has a very restricted range of foods, particularly carrots and chicken drumsticks, he will also binge on cereals at times. Jimmy prefers to stay in the kitchen to eat and is reluctant to join the family in the dining room for meals – even on special occasions.

Organisation

Jimmy can sometimes be a little disorganised. Mum and Dad encourage Jimmy to put things in their correct place, but even when he does Jimmy has difficulty finding them again. Jimmy can be quite particular about putting his items of importance in specific places. If he does so and someone moves them he can become quite cross.

Language and Communication
Oral Language **Level of development:** Jimmy has a good vocabulary and his speech is clear. His sentence structure is still developing and he can on occasion say things that are inaccurate. Jimmy often picks up phrases from films and likes to use these in conversation, but doesn't always use them in the correct context or appropriately. Jimmy is happy to talk about his experiences. He enjoys looking at books, being read to and reading to the other children in the class.
Communication Skills Jimmy's main method of communication is speech and if lost for words he will use gesture. In conversation Jimmy has difficulty making eye contact and he sometimes misses the subtle changes in others tone and expression.
Other/General Comments **Feelings:** Although Jimmy doesn't always respond to others feelings he does recognise sadness and will comfort someone if they are upset.

Environmental and Sensory Influences
Physical Environment Jimmy takes his environment in visually and more recently has been using his sense of smell. He observes situations holistically and is beginning to notice and talk about the things he sees in the environment.
Social Environment Jimmy can become anxious and worried if he hears or anticipates loud noises. If Jimmy loses control he is able to be calmed by being taken away from the situation, comforted and talked to. Jimmy's mum and dad are conscious of the fact that he stands out when he is with children of the same age as he will choose not to socialise with them and plays alone. If Jimmy does play with a friend he will often spend a little time with them then leave them alone so that he can do his own thing. Jimmy does not like it if plans are changed at the last minute and will react badly.
Other/General Comments Points to consider when drawing up the I.E.P: *Sleeping patterns *Eating habits *Socialising with his peers

2.4.2 Example 7 - Recognising and celebrating wider achievement

Tom is in Primary 3 at a small rural primary school. His use of language is inconsistent and he can become frustrated and aggressive at times. He is well supported and completes most tasks but is not always aware of the purpose of activities. One of Tom's particular interests is Trains. When the school needed to buy a new train set they saw an opportunity to incorporate Tom's interest to develop a variety of language and communication skills.

Tom wrote a letter to his headteacher asking if they could buy the train set, found a suitable one in the catalogue, filled in an order form, faxed it to his headteacher (shared headship with another school), and eventually sent away the form. The school recognised the academic and social skills that were naturally involved in the process and recorded Tom's journey in a school display of which he was justifiably proud.

2.4.3 Example 8 - Recognising triggers for behaviour

A primary school child on the autism spectrum was aggressive for the last 30 minutes of every day. His teaching team carried out a Functional Behaviour Analysis (Antecedent, Behaviour Consequence chart) in an attempt to pinpoint why this behaviour was occurring. It became apparent that a reoccurring antecedent to this behaviour was a free choice time for the last 10 minutes of the day. The pupil was desperate to get onto the computer and was worried that another child would choose it first. The teaching team decided to put a rota system in place where a different pupil would get to choose first every day. The pupil now accepts that he may not get on the computer when he does not have first pick. The aggressive behaviour subsided and he is now more open to learning for the last 30 minutes of the day.

2.4.4 The Impact of ASD on Assessment (Grid 3)

The Impact of ASD on Assessment	
Impact of ASD	**Responding to the needs of pupils with ASD**
Links to HGIOS Quality Indicators	
1.1 Improvement in performance 2.1 Learners' experiences 5.3 Meeting learning needs 5.4 Assessment for learning 5.5 Expectations and promoting achievement 5.6 Equality and fairness 5.7 Partnership with learners and parents 5.8 Care, welfare and development	8.1 Partnerships with the community, educational establishments, agencies and employers 8.2 Management of finance for learning 8.3 Management and use of resources and space for learning 8.4 Managing information 9.1 Vision, values and aims 9.2 Leadership and direction
Refer to HMIE *Education for Pupils with Autism Spectrum Disorder* Recommendations 3, 4, 5 and 8	

The Impact of ASD on Assessment	
Impact of ASD	**Responding to the needs of pupils with ASD**
• Pupil may not be able to access standard approaches to assessment.	• Adaptation to assessment process e.g. access to distraction free environment, explanation of ambiguous language, extra time to process and act on or respond to information.
• May have a "spiked" profile meaning that there are inconsistencies in performance of skills and abilities across a range of developmental and curricular areas.	• Do not presume foundation skills are in place. Enable pupils to develop areas of strength whilst being aware of gaps in basic skills and conceptual understanding. Access to a broad and balanced curriculum in keeping with individual profile.
• Transferring skills across environments may be challenging.	• Assess the same competence in a range of settings. Involve and include parents and other relevant agencies in assessment process. Allow time to specifically teach skills in different contexts.

The Impact of ASD on Assessment	
Impact of ASD	**Responding to the needs of pupils with ASD**
• Capacity to access social aspects of school life may need more detailed assessment and support.	• Non curricular areas such as social interaction, play and imagination, independence skills, self awareness and emotional understanding should be incorporated into overall assessment/pupil profile. Capacity to cope with social aspects of school life such as intervals, lunch time and moving from class to class should be considered. These can be significant areas of difficulty and are not peripheral to teaching and learning for pupils with ASD but are central and can potentially impact on learning and well being.
• Inconsistent motivation and engagement may result in misleading outcomes. Pupil may not understand and value the importance of assessment.	• Use pupil's interest to increase engagement in assessment process. Identify what is intrinsically motivating for the pupil as they are unlikely to respond to extrinsic or social motivators. Acknowledge that reasonable adjustment has been made in order to maintain a realistic perspective of the pupil and their skills and competencies.
• Pupil may lack self awareness resulting in difficulties with meaningful involvement in their own learning.	• Support pupil to notice and comment on their own performance and behaviour in relation to specific or agreed targets. Develop and use visual materials to support pupil in recognising and recording their own progress (see examples 1 and 5).

The Autism Toolbox

Part 2
Section 2.5

Individualised Educational Programmes

2.5 Individualised Educational Programmes

Having assessed pupils learning needs in the context of their autism profile an individualised educational programme (IEP) should be developed. The assessment process will have identified areas of difficulty for the pupil, these in turn will have to be prioritised, it would usually be unrealistic and inappropriate to attempt to address all areas at the one time. Each area of priority can then be tackled through specific targets. Pupils on the autistic spectrum will not automatically have an IEP, although most will have some non-curricular targets even if they do not warrant a full IEP.

Two examples of completed IEPs (Exemplars 5 and 6) can be found in the Exemplars folder on the CD Rom.

What is an IEP?

- A set of individualised targets determined by the pupil's strengths and additional support needs
- A collaborative plan incorporating parents, school staff, external agencies, and, when appropriate, the pupil's views
- A detailed plan of strategies resources and staffing to achieve targets
- A method of reviewing targets
- A record of achievement

When is an IEP required?

- No statutory requirement – HOWEVER, there is a statutory requirement to meet the additional support needs of all children, and this would be difficult without a plan
- When existing planning formats cannot reflect the learning needs and achievements of pupils – unmet needs
- When a range of people work with the child, to ensure consistency and improve communication around agreed targets
- When there is a CSP in place

Who writes an IEP?

- AN IEP should be collaborative
- An IEP MUST involve parents
- Class teacher and support staff
- Senior management responsibility
- External agencies

What is included in an IEP?

- General pupil information and details of additional support needs
- Long and short term targets (SMART* targets)
- Curricular and social targets, e.g. sections on social interaction, self awareness, and independence
- Home targets

IEPs should:

- Raise achievement
- Be seen as a working document
- Use a simple format and be jargon free
- Be shared with parents, relevant staff, and where appropriate pupils
- Include pupils' views where appropriate
- Accommodate uneven profile of pupils with ASD
- Be reviewed regularly – at least twice a year
- Be incorporated into other planning formats, e.g. CSP. ASP, PLP, Management plans, ICMP, care plans

* SMART – specific, measurable, achievable, realistic and timed.

2.5.1 Pupil Involvement

Consultation with pupils is becoming an increasingly significant issue in education (Standards in Scottish Schools etc. Act 2000). This has been highlighted in recent documentation such as Building Excellence (Scottish Government, 2007d) and Assessment is for Learning (LTS, SQA, Scottish Executive, 2006). Meaningful involvement of pupils can potentially enhance their learning and enhance experiences for pupils and staff. Pupils on the autism spectrum face particular barriers when it comes to formulating and expressing opinions. It would however be inaccurate to assume that such pupils do not hold opinions. Individuals on the autism spectrum tend towards rigid but often logical patterns of thinking. This can often bring a refreshingly honest perspective but can also result in pupils being viewed as inflexible, pedantic or critical of traditional approaches.

Facilitating the participation of pupils on the spectrum in school matters is an important aspect of an inclusive approach. Adjustments are likely to be required to enable pupils to make their contribution. This will involve forward planning to allow time to adapt processes to ensure pupils have an opportunity to influence their own learning. Strategies outlined in the *Classroom Organisation* section such as use of visual communication tools and social stories (Gray, 2002) will support this.

Some additional things to think about are:

- Discussion with a known and trusted adult to ensure the pupil understands why their views are important
- Use of a visual format for pupils to record their views
- Meetings – explain who will be at the meeting and why
- Clear information about when the pupil will be involved in a meeting and what that will be
- “Permission” to not take part in meetings if they choose
- Use of alternative consultation methods rather then face-to-face meetings (e.g. e-mail)
- A trusted adult to express views on behalf of the pupil if they are not comfortable speaking in a formal meeting
- Follow up after meetings to ensure the pupil is clear about any outcomes and what they mean for the pupil on a day to day basis

The following exemplars are available in the Exemplars folder on the CD Rom

Exemplar 1	- Pupil profile template
Exemplar 2	- Pupil preparation for review meeting
Exemplar 3	- Early Years approaches – Q and A
Exemplar 4	- Management plan – Primary School
Exemplar 5	- Individualised Educational Plan 1
Exemplar 6	- Individualised Educational Plan 2
Exemplar 7	- Additional support planned activities template
Exemplar 8	- Communication Assessment Early Years
Exemplar 9	- Passport template
Exemplar 10	- Completed Passport

2.5.1 The Impact of ASD on Individualised Educational Programmes (Grid 4)

The impact of ASD on Individualised Educational Programmes	
Impact of ASD	**Responding to the needs of pupils with ASD**
Links to HGIOS Quality Indicators	
1.1 Improvements in performance 1.2 Fulfilment of statutory duties 2.1 Learners' experiences 2.2 The school's success in involving parents, carers and families 5.1 The curriculum 5.2 Teaching for effective learning 5.3 Meeting learning needs 5.4 Assessment for learning 5.5 Expectations and promoting achievement 5.6 Equality and fairness	5.7 Partnerships with learners and parents 5.8 Care, welfare and development 6.1 Policy review and development 7.3 Staff development and review 8.1 Partnerships with the community, educational establishments, agencies and employers 8.4 Managing information 9.1 Vision, values and aims 9.3 Developing people and partnerships 9.4 Leadership of improvement and change
Refer to HMIE *Education for Pupils with Autism Spectrum Disorder* Recommendations 3, 4, 5, 7 and 8	

The impact of ASD on Individualised Educational Programmes	
Impact of ASD	**Responding to the needs of pupils with ASD**
• Existing planning approaches and tools may not meet the needs of pupils with ASD.	• In addition to standard curricular areas, social aspects may need to be significantly expanded upon e.g. Personal & Social Development – may need to include areas such as social interaction, self awareness, independence, emotional awareness (see examples 11, 12, 13).
• Likely to need extended and specific supports to access the mainstream curriculum.	• Tasks likely to need differentiation - See section 2.7 on differentiation. Individualised visual communication supports may need to be developed based on assessment profile.
• Social skills will need to be explicitly assessed and taught.	• Liaison with SALT may be required to support social development. Consultation with parents regarding their priorities will be important. Social skills need to be practiced in naturalistic environments. • CPD for school staff in these areas is likely to be needed to enable staff to understand the key issues and to develop appropriate targets and teaching activities.

The impact of ASD on Individualised Educational Programmes	
Impact of ASD	**Responding to the needs of pupils with ASD**
• Unstructured social aspects of the school day will need careful planning.	• Whole school awareness is important. Non teaching staff should be aware of and involved in formulation of targets to meet needs outwith the classroom e.g. Intervals and dining hall etc. Consideration of the whole school environment from the perspective of pupils with ASD will be needed to ensure empathic and supportive responses.
• Transitions across the school day including coming to and leaving school will need careful planning.	• An effective, reciprocal system for home/school communication is needed so that issues relating to identified and agreed targets arising from either environment can be monitored and acted upon. • Liaison with escorts and other adults involved in transporting pupils to and from school may be needed to ensure consistency for key targets. Similarly liaison with any before and after school care providers will also be beneficial.
• Pupils will need support to monitor their own progress and to be actively involved in their own learning.	• Pupils are likely to need time and structured support to prepare a meaningful contribution to the planning and review process (see exemplar 2). Self assessment tools may need adapted to accommodate the thinking and information processing styles of pupils with ASD. Targets should be reinforced daily in the classroom environment with specific target highlighted so the pupil is aware of the focus of their efforts and that the potential to feel overwhelmed is minimised.
• There is likely to be a range of professionals involved in supporting the pupil and their family (see section 4 on Working with Other Agencies).	• Robust systems for ongoing review involving key professionals and the family will be needed. Sufficient time will need to be allocated for staff to prepare for and to be involved in meetings. Parents may need support to be actively involved in meetings, e.g. having any paperwork in advance of the meeting and having sufficient time to express their views within the meeting and being able to bring a supportive friend or advocate with them. Continuous monitoring, review and development of targets should be a shared commitment on the part of all involved adults.

The Autism Toolbox

Part 2
Section 2.6

Classroom Organisation and Classroom Strategies

2.6 Classroom Organisation and Classroom Strategies

2.6.1 Classroom Organisation

The physical environment can make a lot of demands on children and young adults with ASD due mainly to sensory difficulties and problems with central coherence. As with physical, visual or hearing impairment, for children with a communication impairment it is important that reasonable adjustments are made to reduce as many barriers to learning as possible.

> *'for almost any other special need, the classroom only becomes disabling when a demand to perform a given task is made. For the child with autism, disability begins at the door.'*
>
> Hanbury (2007)

Consideration of where children sit is important. There is never enough room in busy mainstream classrooms, and every child is different, but there are a number of basic issues which should be addressed. For example, are they going to be overly distracted if sat by a door or window? Will they be unsettled if they are in a main thoroughfare? Are they seated next to a radiator getting them literally overheated or are they so transfixed by the computer they can't concentrate on anything else?

As a general rule aim for a clutter-free environment to cut down on distraction and confusion. Sometimes it will be appropriate to provide a separate work area for certain pieces of work - this could be their work area, a work station, or office. If pupils do have a separate area to help them focus on work tasks they must also have a space within an appropriate social group rather than 'squeeze them in' when they are joining group activities. This area might be used at times for other pupils who are doing a special piece of work.

Example 9 - Creating a focused work area within a mainstream class

A school with 2 pupils on the spectrum in a P5 class developed the idea of an individualised work station by creating an "office" area within the class. This space was available to all pupils who recognised that they needed a quieter space in which to work. The office was deliberately designed to give the feeling of a "grown up" space using real life office equipment. Pupils were also given the option to wear headphones and listen to music if they wished. Very quickly this resource became a normal, accepted part of the classroom.

Consideration should also be given to social groupings and personalities, ideally providing good social role models. If badly handled, children on the autistic spectrum are often 'wound up', or victimised by peers which creates additional barriers to learning.

Structure and predictability can reduce stress and in some cases challenging behaviour. Where possible create physical structure, either using furniture or even tape or a mark on the floor. Make the function and any accompanying rules of each area as clear as possible, e.g. rules for using computer 1) No-one else is on the computer, 2) work tasks are finished, 3) permission from adult, 4) only for a set time, or a simple open or closed Visual on the computer.

Most children on the autistic spectrum respond positively to a visual timetable, sometimes existing class or group task charts will be enough, but often they require to be individualised (see classroom strategies).

The concept of time can often be difficult for pupils on the autistic spectrum, and they benefit from explicit visual cues or prompts to help them gauge the progress of the day and as they get older to manage their time. If pupils can tell the time a clock is the most obvious Visual. You could incorporate a marker to show clearly when a piece of work should be finished, younger children respond well to kitchen timers and sand timers. There are also a number of timers commercially available aimed at pupils with additional support needs.

The overall working environment can raise numbers of challenges for individuals on the spectrum, both within the classroom and beyond.

A teacher supporting pupils in a secondary school recognised the need to make adjustments to the environment for pupils on the spectrum. Drawing on information from www.autism-in-school.org.uk he constructed an audit tool that has been used to re-organise classrooms. An almost immediate positive effect on pupils has been noted.

Example 10 - Environmental audit (www.autism-in-scotland.org.uk)

Component	Task	Responsibility	Timeline
Are there three clearly delineated areas in classrooms for specific activities (ICT, group work, independent work)			
Is there a 'Quiet Room' for pupils who require time alone during times of stress?			
Is all clutter stored out of sight in designated storage areas?			

Component	Task	Responsibility	Timeline
Do learning areas have clearly designated and well organised and attractive display areas?			
Is there a calm and peaceful environment throughout the ASD resource?			
Do external windows provide adequate lighting but sufficient privacy?			

2.6.2 Classroom Strategies

There are no set answers to working with pupils on the autistic spectrum. Although we have a number of strategies which have been proven to be successful, a careful analysis of the pupil's learning needs must have taken place to understand how ASD will affect each individual pupil's perspective, motivation and preferred ways of working.

> *"..if educationalists try to follow a "recipe", then, they will sooner or later come across a child or a situation where the recipe does not work. Without an understanding of what to do and why, they will find themselves in the same position as the individual with autism: unable to step outside of the learned routine and at a loss how to proceed next."*
>
> Jordan and Powell (1997, preface)

Once you have considered the general physical environment it might be helpful to develop specialised visual supports to support learning in a number of ways. Children and young adults on the autistic spectrum usually respond well to information being presented visually rather than relying on language or verbal instructions, visuals are not just for timetables. Appropriate use of visuals can help children to:

- Predict and prepare for the day's activities, often reducing stress levels
- Organise themselves and materials or resources, reducing the likelihood of confusion or frustration – for pupils and staff
- Introduce and develop an understanding of the concept of time (now, next, finished)
- Work through tasks or common routines independently
- Make choices and express opinions
- Identify and explore feelings
- Reflect on personal experiences and behaviour patterns

Visual Supports - what are they?

Visuals are not just shiny, computer produced, laminated symbols. They should be relevant, motivating, and flexible/transferable. Visual timetables and supports should take account of the pupil's cognitive ability and age. Any of the following can provide visual support:

- Photographs
- Objects
- Magazines
- Drawings
- Commercially made icons
- Words/text
- Timers/calendars
- Video

We all depend on visual supports to some degree or other - diaries, to-do lists, elaborate networks of post-it notes, or shopping lists scribbled on the back of an envelope. The potential for using visual supports is vast, but they should only be used if appropriate and effective and should be regularly reviewed as part of the assessment process. Used indiscriminately they will be at best ineffectual, or in some cases damaging in terms of social development and self esteem.

In some instances the introduction of visual supports can make a significant difference to a pupil's ability to cope with their environment, modify inappropriate behaviours, or work more productively. While it is tempting to think things are 'sorted', removing visual supports too quickly may simply see a return to previous difficulties. Some children, including the most cognitively able, may always need some additional structure or support to organise themselves and be able to access their educational or social environment. (See examples of visual supports, pp 56, 61, 83, 85, 95, 99, 124,151, 208,134 and 143).

Parents and any relevant agencies should have copies of any visuals being used in the class to ensure consistency. Even if a visual is not applicable in the home environment it is always helpful if parents are aware of strategies being used.

Social environment

Having considered the physical environment, staff will also need to plan the social environment and be aware of strategies to support pupils to negotiate the hidden social curriculum (see section 2.8 - Social Curriculum). Staff should, where possible, make social rules or procedures explicit – possibly with a supporting visual. There will also need to be specific preparation or teaching of social skills, and agreed strategies or approaches for repairing social situations which have broken down. There are a number of commercial packages or programmes available, such as Social Use of Language Programme (Wendy Rinaldi, www.wendyrinaldi.com), Socially Speaking (Schroeder, 1998), and Developing Social Interaction and Understanding (Knott and Dunlop, 2007). There are also a wealth of resources and games available to promote social understanding and self esteem which can be accessed through catalogues such as 'Incentive Plus' (www.incentiveplus.co.uk).

Social stories

One of the most commonly used approaches for pupils with ASD is a social stories approach. They are short pieces of writing which enable children to understand information, cues and actions for specific social situations. Social stories describe a specific social situation and often include suggestions for appropriate actions in the future. An important element of the stories is that they help us understand the perspective of children with ASD. Carol Gray, who developed Social Stories™, recommends a specific structure when writing a social story, using different types of sentences, e.g. descriptive, perspective, affirmative or directive. Information around social stories can be found at www.thegraycenter.org.

Social stories should always be individualised. It is highly unlikely you will ever be able to photocopy a social story, as it would not be specific enough to your situation and would bypass the crucial step of considering the social situation from the particular pupil's perspective. Carol Gray emphasises that the process of writing a story can be as important as the product.

Stories are usually written in the first person. They should be non-judgmental and positive, and use vocabulary which is relevant to the child, e.g. story corner/group time/ circle time. Language must also match the pupil's cognitive ability. Stories can be written about any situation - even when it may be a little indelicate - for example, a social story about why we have to wipe our bottoms. As long as they are factual, delivered sympathetically, respectfully, and are helpful.

Parents should have a copy of all social stories, even if it is not pertinent to the home environment to ensure that the pupil's family are aware of social situations being tackled, and are able to reinforce in a range of environments outwith school.

Comic Strip Conversations

Also developed by Carol Gray, comic strip conversations are an excellent method of exploring social situations from different perspectives in a very immediate and visual way. Comic strip stories are discussed and developed with the pupils in a factual non-judgmental way. The adult (or child) talks through a situation illustrating relevant people with matchstick figures. The two key elements of each story is what the involved parties said or did (in a speech bubble), followed by what they were thinking (in a separate thought bubble). The process of understanding what other people are thinking, particularly if it does not seem to match up with what they are saying can be problematic, confusing and at times upsetting for pupils on the autistic spectrum. For example, '*I don't want to play anymore*' could be interpreted as not ever playing again, not playing because they don't like the pupil, or game (which could be just as offensive to a pupil on the autistic spectrum). The reality might be that the child has been playing chases for a while and just wants a rest, or to play something else. Sometimes the relationship between thoughts and actions or words needs to be simply but explicitly discussed with children on the autistic spectrum.

As with all strategies this approach does require time to be tackled effectively. However, it is one of the best ways for adults working with a child on the autistic spectrum to understand the world from their perspective, enabling them to become more perceptive and skilled at responding appropriately. Crucially this type of approach can also prevent secondary behavioural problems and be a constructive means of helping pupils understand the social world.

Understanding Behaviour

Some children with ASD might at times present challenging behaviour. It is crucial to understand that there is no behaviour which is in itself 'autistic', and there is no easy or standardised approach. Perceptions of 'challenging' can vary widely: school staff are not a homogenous group and will have different tolerance levels and interpretations of challenging. However, if unrealistic expectations are imposed on pupils, it is highly likely that they will eventually respond in an unacceptable or challenging manner. Staff must establish the communicative intent of behaviours, viewing problematic situations from the perspective of the pupil on the spectrum, while considering their own interaction style and how it impacts on the pupil.

When dealing with a challenging situation priority must be given to resolving the immediate situation keeping the pupil, peers and staff safe in as dignified a manner as possible. Staff should also consider why the situation arose and what they would do to prevent it happening again. Typically this process might include drawing on some of the strategies mentioned: visuals to provide structure and predictability, adaptations to the environment to limit distractions and sensory sensitivities, or social stories to explore and direct future social interaction. Reward systems may also need to be developed to focus on areas of difficulty, recording and rewarding positive behaviours (see Section 2.7 - Differentiation – Principles and Practicalities). Understanding and responding to pupil behaviour is clearly a complex issue. Helpful resources are highlighted in Section 6 - Resources which is available in Part 3.

2.6.3 Collaborative Working in the Classroom

The need for collaborative working is highlighted in a raft of recent policy guidance and documentation. There can be a tendency to interpret multi-professional collaboration as formal meetings involving external agencies and professionals who are allied to the school. This can involve the teacher engaging with professionals such as speech and language therapists, occupational therapists or educational psychologists and there are likely to be existing, formal procedures to facilitate this. Whilst everyone has an important contribution to make there can be issues in terms of the management and co-ordination of a range of professionals and the information they generate. This is especially true where pupils with complex needs are concerned. However the most vital aspect of collaborative working is that which occurs on a daily basis in the classroom and wider school community, particularly support assistants.

The dynamics of the relationship between the teacher and support assistant is especially important. The support assistant tends to be the adult who has the most prolonged, individual contact with pupils on the spectrum and it is therefore important that they are enabled to make a contribution to the planning and reviewing of pupil support and progress. For pupils on the autism spectrum this will be especially relevant to the social aspects of school life e.g. dinner hall, playground, school transport and lunch/out of school activities.

In order to nurture and facilitate the effective deployment of support assistants there is a role for managers within schools to sensitively monitor and review the activity and involvement of staff in this role. Policies and procedures are required that support the development of the relationship between teachers and support staff, that identify and respond to the need of all staff for CPD in autism spectrum disorders and that ensure appropriate support and responses to staff when they are involved in supporting difficult or challenging behaviour. The National Plan for Autism (NIASA, 2003) recommends that staff who have acquired experience in supporting the complex needs of pupils on the spectrum should be regarded as an asset and consideration should be given to consistency and stability for them and the pupils when allocating staff resources throughout the school.

Support assistants will need guidance to ensure that they are able to fulfil their role in a way that promotes independence, autonomy and self determination for pupils rather than being overprotective or creating a relationship of dependency. This is not to say that establishing trusting and respectful relationships is not to the advantage of the pupil but rather that support will at times need to be subtle rather than overt.

It is important to acknowledge that teachers may feel insecure or unsure about managing and directing another adult within the classroom especially if they are also in the early stages of developing their knowledge of the autism spectrum. Similarly the support assistant may lack confidence to contribute to discussion regarding pupils or may feel unsure of their role. Again, leadership and direction will be required to support staff to establish productive working practices.

2.6.4 The Impact of ASD on Classroom Organisation and Classroom Strategies (Grid 5)

The impact of ASD on Classroom Organisation and Classroom Strategies	
Impact of ASD	**Responding to the needs of pupils with ASD**
Links to HGIOS Quality Indicators	
1.1 Improvement in performance 1.2 Fulfilment of statutory duties 2.1 Learners' experiences 5.2 Teaching for effective learning 5.3 Meeting learning needs 5.4 Assessment for learning 5.5 Expectations and promoting achievement 5.6 Equality and fairness 5.7 Partnership with learners and parents 5.8 Care, welfare and development 7.3 Staff development and review	8.2 Management of finance for learning 8.3 Management and use of resources and space for learning 8.4 Managing information 9.1 Vision, values and aims 9.2 Leadership and direction 9.3 Developing people and partnerships
Refer to HMIE *Education for Pupils with Autism Spectrum Disorder* Recommendations 4, 5, 7 and 8	

The impact of ASD on Classroom Organisation and Classroom Strategies	
Impact of ASD	**Responding to the needs of pupils with ASD**
• Sensory processing differences may cause the pupil to experience stress and anxiety in a range of environments.	• Staff working with the pupil need to accept that these are legitimate and often complex issues that impact on learning and learning behaviour. Staff do not need high level technical knowledge in relation to sensory processing but do need a willingness to adapt advice based on assessed or identified issues that may have a sensory basis.
• Cognitive processing such as Central Coherence difficulties may impact on the pupil's capacity to identify and act upon common environmental cues. Identifying and understanding the appropriate focus of attention may be problematic.	• Pupils may need time to familiarise themselves with the classroom environment and surrounding key areas. • Cupboards and resource areas should be clearly labelled to show content and or function.

The impact of ASD on Classroom Organisation and Classroom Strategies	
Impact of ASD	**Responding to the needs of pupils with ASD**
• Pupils may become overwhelmed by environmental stimuli.	• Pupils may need the opportunity to identify where they feel most comfortable sitting. • Pupils may benefit from access to a quieter, distraction free area in the class, this does not need to be for the sole or permanent use of pupils with ASD but could be an area where any pupil can go to focus on a piece of work (see example 9, p.80).

• Pupils with ASD may appear to be easily and frequently distracted by environmental factors. Such factors may be obvious, uncommon or responses to anticipated events e.g. the bell ringing.	• Pupils with ASD may benefit from having a map of the school so they are clear about how they will move from area to area. This is increasingly important in primary school but will almost certainly be a valuable support in a secondary environment.
	• Pupils may, on occasion need time to withdraw and settle following upset. They may need:
	  • Time to calm down and return to the environment
	  • An explanation of what has occurred
	  • Some aspect of the environment may have to be altered
	• If children are unduly stressed they will be unlikely to be able to learn therefore such approaches are a valid and worthwhile investment of time and are a legitimate strategy to enable learning needs to be met.

• Pupils with ASD may have a poor sense of group culture and group identity and this may be a factor in relation to collaborative working or group tasks.	• Pupils may need a range of prompts including verbal and visual supports in order that the focus of attention is explicit. An environment that is as clutter and distraction free as possible will maximise capacity to concentrate. This does not mean that there should be no visual stimulus present however when pupils are involved in altering their environment e.g. being present when displays are mounted rather than them appearing overnight are more likely to accept and adjust to such change.

The impact of ASD on Classroom Organisation and Classroom Strategies	
Impact of ASD	**Responding to the needs of pupils with ASD**
• Pupils are likely to be more vulnerable to peers who may focus in on unusual social behaviour and who may exploit inappropriate attempts to interact.	• Pupils will need a sensitive and empathic approach to enable them to be meaningfully included in social aspects of learning. An incremental approach may be needed e.g. working with an adult then working in pairs and building to groups. It should be acknowledged that for some pupils this will always be problematic. It may also be sporadic with pupils being able to function in groups for some purposes especially if they are related to specific interests but not for others. This also applies to social aspects of the school day, e.g. lunch times.
• Ritualistic or routine driven behaviour may develop as a compensatory coping strategy if there is an absence of structure and predictability in the immediate and wider environment.	• Staff will need to monitor carefully peer interactions and when necessary intervene to prevent escalation of any issues. Sensitivity will be required so that social attempts by pupils with ASD are not undermined. Any negative targeting of pupils with ASD should be dealt with immediately and be seen as bullying. It may on occasion be necessary to undertake work with peers as well as with the pupil on the spectrum. This work could form part of a PSD topic or programme. Whilst individual, confidential information regarding specific pupils must not be shared a more general approach to discussing diversity and difference may be helpful. It may be beneficial to be proactive in relation to such issues rather than have to formulate approaches when issues arise and the confidence of the pupil with ASD is damaged.
• Concerning behaviours may arise as a result of high levels of stress from prolonged periods in unpredictable or highly socially demanding and confusing settings.	• It is important to observe and assess such behaviour as it may be due to environmental factors that may be relatively easy to adjust. Using an environmental audit tool may assist (see example 10, p 81). It is also important to ascertain if there is sufficient predictability from the child's perspective, if there is sufficient visual communication and if there is a balance in terms of expected demand especially social demand.

The impact of ASD on Classroom Organisation and Classroom Strategies	
Impact of ASD	**Responding to the needs of pupils with ASD**
• Poor understanding of time concepts, including the passage of time, quantifying time and abstract language used around time e.g. later, soon, in a wee while may provoke anxiety.	• Individualised, empathic responses are important. Regular time out or access to time out may be beneficial. Teaching self-regulatory strategies may be important i.e. having supports and strategies in place that enable the pupil to recognise when they are stressed and need to take evasive action. Reasonable adjustments and allowances may need to take place such as not attending assembly or withdrawing from certain subjects that result in stress or having content of such subjects delivered by alternative means. • Concrete markers of time, passage of time, start and finish are required to enable the pupil to orientate themselves across the school day. Language that can be interpreted literally should be avoided - "in a minute" may mean precisely that to a pupil with ASD. Similarly abstract language such as" later" is best avoided, instead use concrete signifiers such as "when lunch is finished" For secondary pupils the timetable should indicate the times when classes will start and finish. Pupils may need specifically taught to accept a more flexible approach to time. Rather than it will happen at 1pm it may help to give parameters e.g. It will happen between ten to and ten past one – this is dependent on individual knowledge of the child as some pupils will find this approach stressful.
• Pupils with ASD are likely to need a high level of repetition of information. This may be due to the way in which information is processed or to a high level of anxiety.	• Staff attitude is important here. The pupil is unlikely to be asking repetitive questions to irritate staff, rather they may have difficulty retaining and recalling information in context or indeed see the relevance of specific information to a context. A concrete record of key information using visual supports if needed is likely to minimise the need for repetitive questions. However if supports are in place such behaviour may be indicative of much deeper rooted stress and anxiety.

The Autism Toolbox

Part 2
Section 2.7

Differentiation – Principles and Practicalities

2.7 Differentiation – Principles and Practicalities

2.7.1 Differentiation

Most teachers have experience of differentiating tasks in a variety of ways to accommodate the learning needs of all pupils in their class, whether they have identified additional support needs or not.

Typically classroom teachers will adapt teaching content in terms of the level of work in response to the pupil's cognitive level or experience. However, there are many other ways of differentiating tasks which can be particularly appropriate for children on the autistic spectrum. Often one of the most important factors is not their cognitive level but their motivation level. Presentation of tasks and recording of information can also be challenging.

Language levels

Pupils with an ASD will have some difficulties around processing language. While it is natural to want to provide a rich language environment for any pupil who has difficulties in this area, sometimes it is necessary to cut down the amount of language used because too much is simply confusing or overwhelming.

Verbal and written instructions should take account of the pupil's language level, where possible removing extraneous or unnecessary language. If verbal instructions have to be repeated reduce the language but keep to the same basic structure rather than completely rephrasing, e.g. 'put your jotter in the finished work tray then come and sit in the book corner', reduced to 'finished work tray then book corner', rather than giving the same instruction in a different way e.g. 'just put it there and come over to join us - we're waiting...'

If work tasks are dependent on language but the actual teaching concept is not, e.g. a problem solving question about division (sharing sweets), pupils may become confused by the language although they are very capable of doing division sums when presented simply. Pupils may also become distracted by irrelevant details, e.g. What type of sweets are they? What if the children don't like those sweets? Does their mummy let them have sweets? and, What about that boy there (at the bottom of the page) - has he to get sweets?...

It is important that pupils learn to interpret information and apply it to functional situations. However, staff need to be clear about what the main teaching point of a lesson is – division or problem solving? It would be unrealistic to introduce the language and problem solving element until the concept of division in a simpler format has been mastered. As with many pupils, it will be easier for children to attempt problem solving activities if they have experience of the situation in a functional context or at least with practical materials before attempting a language laden problem in a textbook or workbook.

Presentation of tasks

Many commercially produced textbooks are designed to be bright, colourful and exciting. However for some children this approach can be distracting, confusing and overwhelming.

In this instance, tasks will need to be simplified: this could be done with a marker or sheet of paper to cover up distracting information. Sometimes tasks might be better transferred to a simpler format – a worksheet, an individual white board, the teaching board or whiteboard, or a computer.

For some children the amount of work on a page can be off-putting and a clear marker of how much of the page should be completed can be helpful. *Occasionally* the adult may have to consider do they need to complete the whole page to demonstrate they understand the concept? Or is it satisfying our need to have a nice finished page of work?

Recording information

Many children with ASD have difficulty producing written work. This can be for a variety of reasons: motivation, fine motor skills, a need for perfection or distractibility. However, this should not prevent them accessing the curriculum, but sometimes it will require flexibility and creativity to reflect their abilities and achievements. Although there will be times when a written piece of work is required there are many alternatives. Below are just a few – you will probably know of others:

- Photographs
- Pre-written labels
- Access to a computer
- Scribing (to varying degrees)
- Magnetic boards and photocopier
- Whiteboards/chalkboards
- Video
- Illustrations/drawings

2.7.2 Motivation

Class teachers often find the task of motivating young people on the autistic spectrum difficult, but it is misleading to suggest that children with ASD cannot be highly motivated. The challenge lies in finding ways to use the interests and particular obsessions pupils are motivated by to channel them towards tasks the adults wish them to attempt. For most children, there *will* be something they are motivated by. If teachers can successfully identify and use these interests, children with ASD can be some of the most focused children in their class.

Children with ASD have special interests that can range from age appropriate through to the obscure.

Throughout this range there is always scope to explore ways of using their interests to motivate them to carry out activities they find challenging. It could be as simple as allowing a child a set time to play with their favourite toy once they have completed a task. This could be presented visually - first task X...then toy - using objects, symbols or text as appropriate. The amount of rewards would be very much dependent on the individual child or difficulty associated with the task.

As well as immediate motivation to complete tasks, teachers can use children's special interests for a variety of other reasons. Systems can be developed to motivate children around academic work, behaviour, communication, and PSD targets. Where possible, teachers should attempt to have pupils with ASD access the school or class reward systems, however, many pupils will be more enthusiastic if the system used has their special interests as a theme or part of an award.

Sometimes special interests might be a little more obscure than a common toy. For example, if a child has a special liking for patterned metal or military leaders, then the reward can be tailored to reflect this. It is often a valuable exercise to spend time with people who know the pupil (and the pupil themselves if appropriate), to identify a list of powerful motivators. It is important that these are pupil led, and may therefore be unusual, for example, historical figures. In this case a reward system that relates the positive choices, attainments and achievements of the child to historical events, may be extremely motivating. A favourite king winning battles, or famous military figure being promoted through the ranks as the child's work is successfully completed, will draw attention to and promote motivation towards tasks and goals set by the adults. Encourage the child to complete objectives within an environment or context which is interesting to them and in which they are comfortable.

Occasionally staff may feel uncomfortable about the nature of some interests, particularly if they are not encouraged in the mainstream population, e.g. Power Rangers, Yugioh cards or football teams. However, in most cases, staff should be confident in utilising this focus sensitively to motivate pupils to complete class work or behave positively. Children who obsess over football league tables may access maths work with questions of how many points for 4 wins and a draw, when they would show no interest in number work otherwise. It is simply a case of identifying what children are driven by and tapping into it in an imaginative and flexible way.

The appearance of a child's work can also be altered to reflect their interests. For some children Thomas the Tank Engine on a work sheet is enough for them to take an interest in work they had no previous motivation to engage with; reading words on train silhouettes (instead of traditional reading words) or maths work presented on a washing machine outline - if it works use it! Likewise, the use of stickers with Dr Who printed on them can be infinitely more rewarding for children with ASD with that particular interest than the kinds of awards, such as special Headteacher Awards, that may motivate typically developing children tuned to the social context.

It is understandable that some staff may see the use of interests as 'giving in', or rewarding challenging behaviour. However, the intention is not to deliver the whole curriculum through the solar system or dinosaurs, but to engage pupils in the learning process and give them opportunities to be successful. If we cannot find a way to engage pupils, there will be no progress at all. The Curriculum for Excellence endorses individualisation in learning using pupil interests (Scottish Government, 2008b).

When developing a reward system, consideration should also be given to the frequency of rewards. Many schools operate a very successful 'Golden time' system, pupils typically getting their reward on a Friday afternoon. For some pupils (not only those on the autistic spectrum) Golden time on a Friday afternoon is not going to get you through a rainy Tuesday morning, therefore staff need to consider what is a realistic block of time for pupils to sustain a particular behaviour or pace of work before receiving a tangible recognition of this. Rewards might need to be given daily or even more frequently, perhaps splitting the day into three blocks which should gradually be extended to longer blocks of time.

Where possible, rewards should be earned in a flexible way: points being accrued for particular pieces of work, social interaction or targeted behaviours and these could be 'weighted' depending on level of difficulty. It is best to avoid an 'all or nothing' approach' – why bother to try any more if you know you have lost your reward already?

Be prepared to revise reward systems regularly. Pupils' interests will change appropriately or otherwise as they develop, and interest levels will fluctuate. Involve pupils in their own rewards and give them responsibility for sourcing or suggesting rewards. Finally the ideal situation is to arrive at a point where self-motivation takes over, and rewards can be phased out altogether.

2.7.3 The Impact of ASD on Differentiation (Grid 6)

The Impact of ASD on Differentiation	
Impact of ASD	**Responding to the needs of pupils with ASD**
Links to HGIOS Quality Indicators	
1.1 Improvement in performance 2.1 Learners' experiences 5.1 The curriculum 5.2 Teaching for effective learning 5.3 Meeting learning needs 5.4 Assessment for learning 5.5 Expectations and promoting achievement 5.6 Equality and fairness 5.7 Partnership with learners and parents 5.8 Care, welfare and development	8.2 Management of finance for learning 8.3 Management and use of resources and space for learning 8.4 Managing information 9.1 Vision, values and aims 9.2 Leadership and direction
Refer to HMIE *Education for Pupils with Autism Spectrum Disorder* Recommendations 3, 4, 5 and 8	

The Impact of ASD on Differentiation	
Impact of ASD	**Responding to the needs of pupils with ASD**
• Pupils on the autism spectrum may present with an uneven profile of abilities.	• Assessment will be required to determine the appropriate level of academic tasks. It will be important not to assume competence in one area will mean comparable ability at all levels. This may make for a more protracted approach to assessment but is likely to result in a more comprehensive profile of strength and need.
• Core difficulties with language and the extraction of implied or intended meaning can be a barrier to accessing standard curriculum materials.	• Review teaching materials for language that is ambiguous or could be interpreted on a literal level. • Ensure that the purpose of the task is explicit and that it is not lost in extraneous detail or complex language. • Ensure there is a match between the pupil's language ability and the language used. • Bear in mind that some pupils on the spectrum may have a high level of understanding of technical language but find "carrier" language confusing. This will be particularly relevant to problem solving tasks and in active learning contexts.

The Impact of ASD on Differentiation	
Impact of ASD	**Responding to the needs of pupils with ASD**
• Materials that are overly visually stimulating or that contain superfluous visual information may be confusing or distracting.	• When necessary ensure that work is presented in such a way that the focus of attention is appropriate. This will be determined by observation of how pupils interpret materials and instructions/tasks.
• The boundaries of tasks may be confusing. Pupils may have difficulty getting started or knowing when to stop.	• The beginning and end of tasks may need to be highlighted. This can be achieved by: • Use of timers e.g. sand timers, kitchen timers or a clock with a marker to show when the task will be finished. • Visual markers located in work e.g. “Start” and “stop” or green lights and red lights or arrows to indicate the beginning and the end of exercises. • A box that indicates when work is finished embedded into work may be useful. e.g. ‘Finished’. • Some pupils may benefit from a physical boundary superimposed on the task to make it clear to them what they are supposed to be working on.
• Skills taught in class may not automatically be transferred into a functional context.	• Investing time to practice skills in situ will be beneficial. Teaching the same skill in a variety of contexts may be required. Using real practical materials e.g. using real coins when teaching money values. • Be creative with opportunities around the school to practice skills e.g. buying pencils; snack; reading for information - timetable, instructions; taking on tasks in the office; enterprise projects etc. All of this is likely to be underway for all pupils. Adjustment coupled with a creative approach will maximise the benefit to pupils who are on the spectrum.

The Impact of ASD on Differentiation	
Impact of ASD	**Responding to the needs of pupils with ASD**

• Recording information can be challenging in terms of quality and quantity. Reasons for this include:
  • A need for work to look perfect. This may be due to a tendency for rigid/ inflexible thinking.
  • Fine motor and or sensory issues may impact on the quality of written work due to the over or under exertion of pressure applied.
  • A lack of intrinsic motivation may inhibit the quantity of work produced. A pupil who feels they have mastered a skill may see no purpose or benefit to them in evidencing competence.
	• It will be important to consider whether it is necessary to have written evidence. If so individual motivators may need to be used to encourage the pupil to produce work that reflects their ability.
	• For pupils who tend towards perfectionism, long term approaches to address understanding that everyone makes mistakes should be ongoing.
	• If written evidence is not required consider alternatives such as:
	  • Photographs
	  • Pre-written labels
	  • Access to a computer
	  • Scribing (to varying degrees)
	  • Magnetic boards and photocopier
	  • Whiteboards/chalkboards
	  • Video
	  • Illustrations/drawings

• Autism may overlap with other conditions.	• An occupational therapy assessment may be required for pupils whose motor skills are a consistent source of concern.

• Motivation to engage with tasks is dependent on many factors including:
  • Purpose
  • Interest/experience
  • Tangible outcomes
	• Motivators will vary significantly for individuals with ASD. Consider observing to find what will motivate a pupil in any given situation as this may also vary. Initially motivators are usually highly personal and families will often be able to provide helpful information about their own family member.

The Autism Toolbox

Part 2
Section 2.8

The Social Curriculum

2.8 The Social Curriculum

Kanner (1943) described autism as a disturbance of affective contact. Affect is about how people relate one to another, how we identify, process and act on feelings and emotions. For most typically developing people there is an innate drive for social contact that is evident from the very beginning of life (Hobson, 1993).

Children with ASD do not develop social skills and social competence in the same way as their typically developing peers. It is more usual for children across the autism spectrum to accumulate social knowledge by employing an intellectual rather than an innate approach. In other words they have to systematically learn that which most children learn experientially and developmentally. Responding to the need for a social curriculum for pupils with ASD is an essential component of successful inclusion in any setting. By recognising the value of meaningful social learning, schools will be enabling pupils with ASD to function in and contribute effectively to their own communities. They are also meeting their responsibility to ensure an equitable approach to supporting pupils to attain in the 4 main competencies that are central to Curriculum for Excellence, i.e. successful learners, confident individuals, responsible citizens and effective contributors.

Smith Myles and Simpson (2001) refer to the “hidden curriculum” that is the skills that are not specifically taught but there is an expectation that everyone will have or very quickly develop when they come to school. These skills are numerous and diverse and include:

- Classroom conforming behaviours such as being motivated to please the teacher. Picking up on social cues from others e.g. sitting when they sit, working in groups, engaging in collaborative and shared learning.
- Identifying a hierarchy of social behaviour e.g. behaviour in the classroom is different from the playground and is different again at home or travelling to and from school.
- Playground conforming behaviours including peer pleasing behaviours such as using particular language, engaging in common topics of conversation, knowing what is “cool”/ “uncool.” Knowing how to identify bullies and bullying behaviour. Recognising and acting on friendship signals. Knowing how to break into a group. Knowing when it is best not to be part of the group.
- Community based behaviours such as knowing how to conduct oneself across a range of setting e.g. swimming pool, café or shops.
- Issues can range from simple to complex. Within the school environment pupils are likely to need support to know where to stand, how to use intervals, how to line up or queue for lunch. Equally it is likely that pupils will need support to understand and develop interaction with their peer group. This will be relevant regardless of the age of the pupil, it is important not to assume that an older child or young person will be or indeed should be

able to demonstrate age appropriate social skills. Pupils with ASD do not always learn from accumulated experience.

- Repeated exposure to challenging and stressful situations may potentially impact on the child's well being and also their capacity to learn. It is therefore important to assess level of skill and ability and to set targets accordingly to support social development. It is also important that exposure to such situations is commensurate with the current level of skill.

Diversity comes in many forms and there are likely to be aspects of social learning that are common to children who are not on the spectrum. The profound and pervasive impact of social interaction deficits cannot be overlooked for pupils on the spectrum as they are fundamental to sustained attainment within their education setting.

(Smith Myles and Andreon, 2001)

Example 11 - Promoting peer awareness / buddies

A one hour Personal and Social Education (PSE) lesson was given to secondary pupils attending an ASD base by ASD base staff on different learning approaches, communication challenges and how to help each other (using worksheets, group work and brainstorming). This aimed to develop:

- Peer social interactions during break and lunch times
- Relevant social skills
- Social chat
- Acceptance as part of the year group

Members of the peer group were invited to join base pupils at lunch and break times. A range of resources such as board games and computer games were provided for use. Buddies were used to accompany pupils from the base outside into playground instead of staff member. Training was provided to buddies to help them understand the difficulties pupils from the base may have. Additionally buddies were invited to join outdoor learning days to develop their social skills further and deepen friendships. There is now a regular group of peer group buddies attending the base daily. All pupils are comfortable in each others company and there are regular interactions. Pupils from the base are very popular in classes and are able to work well with buddies. Peer support develops pupils' confidence and independence and encourages positive self esteem allowing supporting adults to withdraw.

Future developments include reviewing the material delivered with the buddies and lessons on hidden disabilities to be linked in with S1 PSE programme.

Example 12 - Developing social confidence- reflected in IEP targets

Gary is a Primary 4 pupil with Asperger's Syndrome. He is coping very well with the academic demands of school but is extremely passive. He will not volunteer information and, if asked directly, he will respond very quietly and uncomfortably. Staff have organised for Gary to take a message to an identified person every day. Staff have been pre-warned and asked not to make it too easy for Gary by anticipating or 'de-coding' the message for him. IEP aims associated with Gary's task are:

- Entering identified areas confidently
- Gaining the adult's attention appropriately
- Conveying messages clearly and confidently
- Listening to and remembering the response
- Ending conversation appropriately
- Delivering a response back to teacher

Example 13 - Visiting a local arts centre with buddy support

A "buddy system" has been developed by an education support service. The service has two class bases attached to mainstream primary schools. Intensive group support is provided as is outreach support for pupils who are managing in their local mainstream school. The class bases are divided roughly into an early years (nursery – P3) and an upper primary group (P4-7). The children attending these bases all have some contact with their local mainstream school.

The buddies who are in P5 - 7 'apply' for the position and attend meetings. They also have a buddy booklet which explains what autism is and how best to be a friend, as well as the chance to read simple published material on autism. This example demonstrates how the use of buddies was developed to include a variety of activities rather than the usual playground support. Access to a local arts centre for expressive arts provided an opportunity for buddies to be involved.

Aims were to:

- Provide the pupils with a new learning experience in a different environment from the classroom
- Enhance the children's experience of relating and interacting with others
- Listen and respond through the medium of music and movement
- Promote a sense of enjoyment and well-being through positive relationships with peers

Each pupil on the autism spectrum was accompanied by a buddy. The theme for the day was 'Friends Together'. Planning for the day involved collaboration between school staff, centre staff and visiting specialists. Preparations to support the communication of pupils on the spectrum such as taking and using photographs of the venue, compiling schedules for the day to provide predictability and writing social stories were undertaken. The outcome was a positive day enjoyed by all. A key point was that pupils were supported mainly by peers rather than adults. Using a natural approach resulted in benefits to all participants. The event has provided a foundation on which to build more opportunities to develop the buddy role.

It is known that children and young people with ASD are vulnerable to being singled out in the peer group. It is therefore important to consider the impact of autism on both bullying and emotional well-being as part of the social curriculum.

2.8.1 The Impact of ASD on the Social Curriculum (Grid 7)

The Impact of ASD on the Social Curriculum	
Impact of ASD	**Responding to the needs of pupils with ASD**
Links to HGIOS Quality Indicators	
1.1 Improvements in performance Fulfilment of statutory duties 2.1 Learners' experiences 2.2 The school's success in involving parents, carers and families 5.1 The curriculum 5.2 Teaching for effective learning 5.3 Meeting learning needs 5.4 Assessment for learning 5.5 Expectations and promoting achievement 5.6 Equality and fairness 5.7 Partnerships with learners and parents 5.8 Care, welfare and development	6.1 Policy review and development 6.2 Participation in policy and planning 7.2 Staff deployment and teamwork 7.3 Staff development and review 8.1 Partnerships with the community, educational establishments, agencies and employers 8.3 Management of resources and space for learning 8.4 Managing information 9.1 Vision, values and aims 9.2 Leadership and direction 9.3 Developing people and partnerships 9.4 Leadership of improvement and change
Refer to HMIE *Education for Pupils with Autism Spectrum Disorder* Recommendations 3, 4, 5, 6, 7 and 8	

The Impact of ASD on the Social Curriculum	
Impact of ASD	**Responding to the needs of pupils with ASD**
• Social skills needed to access learning opportunities are likely to need purposeful teaching.	• Assessing social as well as academic skills is essential as is recognising the validity of teaching such skills and recognising that they are vital to enable pupils to access more formal learning. This is important at all stages i.e. from nursery through to secondary and indeed further and higher education.
• Social knowledge may be out of step with age or other cognitive abilities.	• A sound awareness of ASD in general and how it impacts on individual pupils is needed for staff to recognise and appreciate the significant impact of impairments in social interaction. Impairments can be very obvious but may also be quite subtle. Social expectations should be in line with current capacity rather than expected capacity based on the child's or young person's age.

The Impact of ASD on the Social Curriculum	
Impact of ASD	**Responding to the needs of pupils with ASD**
	• Specific strategies are likely to be needed across a range of contexts • Involving the pupil as much as possible will enable staff to take account of what is motivating for the pupil e.g. it may be important to the pupil to attend a youth club as this is what peers are doing.

• Transferring social skills from one context to another is likely to be problematic.	• It will be important for staff to understand that generalising difficulties are associated with ASD and to recognise that pupils are likely to need direct teaching and support to enable them to use skills in a range of contexts. Pupils will be supported by:
	  • Staff accepting this as a feature of their ASD.
	  • Maximising opportunities for social learning that takes place in situ.
	  • Modelling the expected social behaviour.
	  • Developing appropriate peer support systems such as a 'buddy' system.
	  • Using visual supports to prepare the pupil for new social experiences.
	  • Providing a named and accessible member of staff to support the pupil emotionally when social situations go wrong.
	  • Providing support to enable the pupil to reflect on social situations that have gone wrong and to develop alternative strategies or coping mechanisms. This is likely to require use of a range of strategies that use visual (see p 83) or cognitive approaches.
	  • Using information from previous teaching staff, family members and other involved professionals may be helpful in forming pro-active or preventative strategies.

• Pupils with ASD may make no distinction between how they interact with adults and how they interact with peers. Indeed the pupil may perceive the adults in the setting are more like peers than the other pupils.	• Staff may need support to ensure they do not take the pupil's communication style personally. • Whole school education regarding diversity may help minimise perceptions of other pupils that an individual child "gets away" with particular behaviour that would not be tolerated if offered by other pupils. This does not mean identifying any individual pupil but rather advocates an ethos where pupils are treated equally but individually.

The Impact of ASD on the Social Curriculum	
Impact of ASD	**Responding to the needs of pupils with ASD**
• Pupils with ASD, particularly more able individuals, often have a desire for friendship but lack knowledge and experience of the incremental and complex way in which friendships develop. This can render them socially vulnerable in a number of ways: • They can be vulnerable from more streetwise pupils who may encourage them to be disruptive in order to "earn" a place in a group. • They can be more vulnerable to bullying as they are unable to read the predatory signals of children who engage in bullying. • They are unlikely to be able to generate a range of strategies to enable them to disassociate with individuals who are taking advantage of them. • They may not recognise that they have to report acts of bullying in order to seek support. Added to this they may be unclear about who may be in a position to help them.	• Anti-bullying guidance may need to be differentiated in order to be more accessible for pupils on the spectrum. • Pupils with ASD may need individualised support in order to recognise such behaviour in others. • Pupils are likely to benefit from having a nominated adult or indeed an adult they identify to approach when they feel uncomfortable. Staff may need to initiate support as some pupils would not take the initiative to discuss problems even if they are quite extreme. • Pupils may need to be purposefully taught a range of strategies for removing themselves from situations – such strategies are likely to be helpful to all children. • Pupils may need playground or street language translated for them as there is a tendency towards literal and formal use of language. • A safe haven or retreat within the school may be useful when pupils are feeling overwhelmed or uncomfortable.

The Impact of ASD on the Social Curriculum	
Impact of ASD	**Responding to the needs of pupils with ASD**
• Pupils with ASD are likely to interpret language on a literal level. Added to this there is a tendency for logical, sometimes rigid interpretation of rules. Social behaviour may therefore be very inflexible with some responses being perceived by adults as belligerence. Such pupils are frequently exactly right on a logical level but extremely inappropriate on a social level.	• Clubs and interest groups are likely to provide a place where pupils with ASD can socialise and also shine in terms of their knowledge and or ability. • Again it is important not to take certain responses personally. Staff working with pupils with ASD need to be aware of their own non verbal and verbal language. They may feel their authority is challenged and may feel undermined by the pupil. It is important to reflect on such responses within the context of understanding the impact of ASD on the pupil. It may be beneficial to set out rules, expectations and required standards of behaviour from the outset. Of all the pupils in the class those with ASD are the most likely to conform. It will however be difficult for pupils to detect implied meaning therefore clear and explicit instruction is likely to be needed.

2.8.2 The Impact of ASD on Bullying

Case example of a teenager (15 year old female) with Asperger's Syndrome:

… "I've been bullied so much I'm too anxious to go to school".

(Robinson, 2007)

Although there are no such comprehensive figures for Scotland on the number of school children with autism and Asperger's Syndrome who are bullied in school, a National Autistic Society survey of 1,400 families in England and Wales, the largest ever survey carried out on autism and education, found that over 40% of children on the autistic spectrum had been bullied at school (Reid and Batten, 2006). This is an average taken across establishments with the rate being highest in mainstream schools. In Scotland it has been reported that over a third of children with autism have been bullied at school (Batten and Daly, 2006). In another recent study, 90% of parents surveyed reported that their child with Asperger's Syndrome had been bullied at school within the past year (Little, 2002).

Of course those with an Autism Spectrum Disorder (ASD) are not the only children who experience bullying, however, there are aspects of the condition that leave children with the diagnosis particularly vulnerable to bullying (Robinson, 2005). Having deficits in the core areas of social communication, social interaction and social imagination may mean that children with ASD are more likely to stand out in the school playground because of their unconventional social behaviour, particularly as they get older and social interactions become more complex. These children, who can find it difficult to socialise anyway because of their ASD and the unstructured and social nature of playtime, can become isolated by their peers because they appear different. Initiating interactions, gaining social feedback and sustaining ongoing friendships often require supports, ongoing adaptive strategies and monitoring to facilitate success with relationships.

As previously outlined children with ASD can have difficulty interpreting facial expressions, intonation of voices and implied meaning, body language and often interpret others' language literally. These factors, coupled with an often poor ability to resolve conflict or cope with uncomfortable emotional states, mean that children with ASD might be over sensitive to other children 'having a laugh' with them, resulting in over-reaction from the child with ASD. This can result in the pupil feeling rightly or sometimes wrongly paranoid that others are making fun of them. Paranoia can result from reality or it can sometimes stem from misinterpretation of others intentions. Victimisation can occur if others sense their vulnerability or if they display extreme behavioural responses that others find amusing. Emotional immaturity coupled with odd behavioural responses can sometimes alienate or amuse their peers whilst exasperating their teacher. Alternatively children with ASD might not realise when they are being teased or bullied, or might believe that their experience is the same as everyone else's.

A case example of a teenager (16 year old male) with Asperger's Syndrome who had recently self disclosed his awareness of difficulties with understanding others (an example of possible theory of mind or interpersonal difficulties):

"People would say things to me and I wouldn't know if they were being serious, ... I never knew if they were joking with me or not."

(Robinson, 2006)

Other children can be quick to pick up on the often explosive responses of children with ASD and seek to provoke this reaction from the child, although the instigators have sufficient insight and proficient communication skills to cover their tracks. Due to difficulty understanding other children's motives, perspectives or understanding that their 'friends' may say one thing and think another, children with ASD can appear trusting and be vulnerable to peer manipulation. These children may be exploited for personal belongings or might be 'dared' to do things their peers suggest.

A case example of a teenager (14 year old male) with Asperger's Syndrome:

"I'm considered popular at school because during my first week I lost it and did a Ned Flanders impersonation and since then I'm popular because the other kids say "go on and do that funny thing again" and I say 'No!"

(Robinson, 2007)

This comment demonstrates how the intentions of others are not necessarily understood or can even be misinterpreted. The vulnerability of 'losing it' may actually draw attention to the different reactions to stress displayed by some people with an ASD. These different reactions may then lead to further episodes of bullying. Endeavouring to teach pupils with an ASD to understand other peoples' intentions is an essential part of support. This would underpin their ability to consider that sometimes words are not necessarily all they seem. It should however also be recognised that the responsibility to combat bullying should not solely be placed on the pupil with ASD, but intervention strategies should promote whole school responses as well as providing supports to the pupil in the areas of particular need that arise as an impact of ASD.

A case example of a parent of a teenager with Asperger's Syndrome:

"We had a visit from the Police because my son had used a racial slur towards a girl in his school. He didn't even know what the word meant. He said he was just copying the others, but he was the only one that admitted it when the teacher asked him."

(Scottish Society for Autism (SSA) RU: teen parent training attendee, 2007)

It must be recognised that children with ASD are not always without fault. They may indeed be annoying to other pupils, but their ability to behave in a more socially appropriate way or recognise and change their 'annoying' behaviour is doubtless hindered by their disability. They might repeat words without fully understanding the meaning of the words or the impact of words and behaviour on other children, due to their difficulty with Theory of Mind (understanding the thoughts, feelings and beliefs of others as different from their own). Children with ASD might be capable of enjoying mischievous behaviour, they lack the skills of not getting caught, of being mischievous at the right times in the right measure and of lying about it when questioned that other typically developing children can utilise.

The behaviour seen in all children, including those on the spectrum, resulting from being bullied can be varied, including refusing school, self-harm, decline in school performance, becoming withdrawn, low self-esteem, and even talk of suicide or vengeful thoughts. These experiences can result from incidents of prolonged bullying and it can be viewed as a typical response. Many children do experience bullying. There are additional considerations however in relation to the impact of ASD. The recognition that you are a target of bullying may need to be taught. Bullying involves the intentions; verbal expressions and physical actions of others directed towards you and these all require interpretation. As has been identified previously interpreting social and communicative intent is a particular area of difficulty. Teaching the abstract and more overt signs of bullying may be a useful means of raising understanding.

A case example of a parent of two sons with autism, one in and one approaching transition to mainstream secondary school -

> *"He's not looking forward to secondary, because of his brother's experience: [A] was in class and he jumped up when another boy stuck a pencil in his hand. [A] got in trouble because he was making loads of noise, but he never thought to tell the teacher what had happened before that."*

(SSA, Advisory case, 2008)

This illustrates one aspect of the difficulties people with ASD face in relation to the pragmatics of communication (i.e. knowing that you can explain your behaviour to others).

Whilst whole school policies and approaches to bullying may be equally applicable to, and should take account of, children with ASD and typically developing children alike, teachers and practitioners should be aware that children with ASD are particularly vulnerable to bullying and lack the skills to recognise and deal with it. Bullying and teasing are major barriers to children with autism and Asperger's Syndrome (Barnard, Prior and Potter, 2000; Peacock, Forest and Mills, 1996). A NAS survey of teachers across two local authorities in Scotland (Barnard, Broach, Potter and Prior, 2002) found that many teachers ranked the prevention of teasing and bullying as an important intervention in order to secure successful inclusion. Approaches which place the onus on the child to take responsibility for dealing with bullying, or rely on the child's peer group, should be adopted with caution in the case of autism as such approaches will not play to the child with ASD's strengths.

Although methodological issues regarding research evidence are not of concern here there are research findings proposed regarding the longer term impact of bullying and social isolation. One particular research study found that typically developing children who experience bullying are subjected to an increased risk of developing low self esteem, increased levels of anxiety and depression and increased social isolation (Hodges, Malone and Perry, 1997; Olweus, 1992; Stewart, Barnard, Pearson et al, 2006). Furthermore, some evidence suggests that children without friends may be at risk of delay in social and emotional development, low self-esteem and the development of anxiety and depression in later life (Hay, Payne and Chadwick, 2004). It could be proposed that having friends can act as a preventative measure to low self-esteem and mood disorders (Kim, Szatmari, Bryson, Streiner and Wilson, 2000; Attwood, 2007).

A case example a teenager (15 year old female) with Asperger's Syndrome:

"I just want a friend I can look after… I've had friends but when friends fall out they make up, but no one makes up with me."

(Robinson, 2007)

2.8.3 The Impact of ASD on Bullying (Grid 8)

The impact of ASD on Bullying	
Impact of ASD	**Responding to the needs of pupils with ASD**
Links to HGIOS Quality Indicators	
1.1 Improvement in performance 2.1 Learners' experiences 5.1 The curriculum 5.2 Teaching for effective learning 5.3 Meeting learning needs 5.4 Assessment for learning 5.5 Expectations and promoting achievement 5.6 Equality and fairness 5.7 Partnership with learners and parents 5.8 Care, welfare and development	6.1 Policy review and development 6.2 Participation in policy and planning 7.2 Staff deployment and teamwork 7.3 Staff development and review 8.1 Partnerships with the community, educational establishments, agencies and employers 8.4 Managing information 9.1 Vision, values and aims 9.2 Leadership and direction 9.3 Developing people and partnerships 9.4 Leadership of improvement and change
Refer to HMIE *Education for Pupils with Autism Spectrum Disorder* Recommendations 3, 4, 5 and 8	

The impact of ASD on Bullying	
Impact of ASD	**Responding to the needs of pupils with ASD**
• Core difficulties in social relatedness and understanding will often have a significant impact on the person. For example a pupil with an ASD is unlikely to be socially motivated to fit into the crowd or follow fashion trends: such a pupil may not be motivated by the same types of things as other pupils.	• Assess and develop self-awareness skills in areas related to their vulnerabilities. There are numerous practical resources to help in this area; there are also specific interventions developed to support this area of functioning (Section 6 Resources 11, 16, 25, 26).
• They may like things that seem 'odd' to other pupils and teachers. This can cause them to 'stand out' in a crowd and they can then be susceptible to bullying in response to their difference.	• Developing alternative opportunities, such as 'safe communities' within the school (examples of these can be chess clubs, library or a base to have breaks and lunch).
• There are challenges within the social context resulting from interpersonal engagement, processing the social meaning and awareness of others perspectives.	• Provide social skills training opportunities, but be aware of the limitations of generalising these skills. (Use this as a means of raising the pupil's self-awareness or as an informative informal assessment to guide strategies of support).

The impact of ASD on Bullying	
Impact of ASD	**Responding to the needs of pupils with ASD**
• Difficulty interpreting unspoken meanings behind words can result in the pupil being vulnerable to the intentions of others. Pupils with ASD can often become 'targets' as their social naivety can be very apparent.	• Teach 'signs of bullying' so that the pupil is aware of what behaviours indicate bullying. • Ensure the school anti-bullying policy specifically mentions ASD and the response to be taken to incidents and bullying behaviour. Respectme national anti-bullying service can support the development of and refreshment of policies and provide training for staff. • Help the pupil to understand the school's anti-bullying policy. • Provide 'assertiveness training' but be aware of the possible impact of inflexible thinking and that the pupil may rigidly apply a set response in a variety of different contexts. Additionally, they may not be able to initiate this response in a social situation. Continue to monitor and adapt your support strategies and provide visual supports to augment their learning.
• A pupil with ASD may have a single minded focus on developing friendships. They may desperately want a friend and can misinterpret kindness for friendship and become attached to someone who does not consider them a friend. Inflexibility of thought and a lack of appreciation of the others feelings may result in rejection.	• Consider providing a 'buddy system' or someone who can 'look out' for them and report any situation that they feel are of concern for the person.
• A pupil with ASD may be motivated to 'fit in' with the crowd, but lack the social awareness that they are being 'exploited' by others. Some people engage in 'anti-social' activity.	• Provide visually timetabled 'social translation' sessions. This can provide an opportunity within the day for the pupil to discuss situations they may not have understood or that have been picked up as social misunderstandings by teachers.

2.8.4 The Impact of ASD on Emotional Well-being

'What if an individual cannot explain their emotional or physical experiences? What if, in fact, they are detached from such experiences because they have not been able to gather the information from their senses, experience and comprehension of such experiences? ... This means that I and many other individuals with ASD are prone to high levels of anxiety, but cannot even express this in the way that the neuro-typically developing population can. Instead, we develop inappropriate behaviours, skin irritations, aggressiveness, paranoia, social phobias and others, inabilities to concentrate as well as the typical physical expressions that accompany anxiety."

(Lawson, 2001, p.104)

If we are to consider emotional wellbeing, then consideration should first be given to health and mental health. The definition embraced by the World Health Organization (WHO) of 'health' as referring to "physical, mental, and social well-being" enables us to see how this simple term could elude people with an Autism Spectrum Disorder (ASD). By this very definition the profile of abilities present for all persons with an ASD may well impinge on the state of their health. The primary social aspect of their condition appears to place the person diametrically opposed to healthy wellbeing as they struggle to cope with the basic social nature and social demands of our socially oriented society.

Although it is claimed that it may not be possible concisely to define mental health (Public Health Institute of Scotland, 2003), it is however deemed necessary to understand some of the factors which make up a person's 'mental health' or 'mental well-being.' After a review of the literature however, it is possible to establish a definition of mental health that is quite commonly used:

'The ability to develop psychologically, socially, emotionally, intellectually and spiritually' as well as the ability to, 'initiate, develop and sustain mutually satisfying relationships, use and enjoy solitude, become aware of others and empathise with them, play and learn, develop a sense of right and wrong and to face and resolve problems and setbacks satisfactorily and learn from them.'

(Edwards, 2003)

With this definition of mental health being so fundamentally reliant on social and emotional development, the challenges faced by each person with an ASD is immediately apparent. As has been outlined previously social relatedness presents challenges in that the person may not be socially motivated or derive the same social desire or feedback from social interactions with others. Contrary to the 'socially programmed' neuro-typical population (a term created within the autism field to represent non ASD thinking people), many people with ASD find the presence of others confusing and the need for interplay between self and other has a tendency to provoke anxiety. Dialogue between people can become stressful often being unable to initiate or engage in reciprocal interactions. They may misinterpret others intentions sometimes placing themselves in vulnerable positions due to their social naivety and their inability to 'read people'.

Case example taken from dialogue with a parent of a teenager (13 year old male) with Asperger's Syndrome:

"It initially began with him hiding from people he knew in the street, but now he has become so fearful of meeting anyone he knows outside the house he won't go out. Now he refuses to leave the house, only to go to school. He doesn't join the family to go on outings or even to do everyday family things like shopping."

(SSA, Advisory Case, 2007)

It was 'Towards a Healthier Scotland' (Scottish Office, 1999) that outlined the national priority agenda for improving Scotland's mental health. The Scottish Needs Assessment Programme (SNAP) (2000) recommended that children's mental health and wellbeing should be "mainstreamed'. In 2001, the Scottish Executive's National Programme for Improving Mental Health and Well-Being was established. Following on from this came the strategic framework for health improvement 'Improving Health in Scotland: The Challenge' (Scottish Executive, 2003a). The need for this came from emerging figures showing that around 125,000 young people under the age of 19 have mental problems which cause them daily difficulties in living (Public Health Institute of Scotland 2003). A further report states that 'one in five children and young people in Scotland will suffer from clinically defined mental health problems during their school career' (Edwards, 2003). This amounts to ten per cent of children aged between five and fifteen years of age experiencing clinically defined mental health problems. More recently a new policy document 'Towards a Mentally Flourishing Scotland' (Scottish Government, 2007e) has been published. An action plan on this is expected.

If we look at the impact of mainstreaming from the experiences of those on the autism spectrum that have accessed mainstream community and education, the figures relating to mental health appear quite alarming. The current research indicates that 65% of adolescents with Asperger's Syndrome have a secondary mood disorder, the most common being anxiety disorder (Ghaziuddin et al, 1989; Russell and Sofronoff, 2004). The prevalence of depression is also high, to such an extent that Attwood (2007) proposes that people with Asperger's Syndrome may be vulnerable to depression, with some findings claiming one in three adults develop clinical depression (Tantum, 1988; Tantum, 2000; Wing 1981). Some research has discovered that 25% of adults with Asperger's Syndrome also have clear clinical signs of Obsessive Compulsive Disorder (OCD) (Russell, Mataix Cols, Anson and Murphy, 2005). Often OCD can become confused with repetitive stimulation or a preoccupation of a narrowed focused interest. People with an ASD often engage in a focused interest for numerous reasons, examples of such are simply for the pleasure or the calming effect these can have when faced by stressful situations. It should be recognised that not all pre-occupations of idiosyncratic interests are a sign of OCD. However, the ability to control the amount of time devoted to ones special narrowed focused interest can be indicative of the development of OCD (Baron-Cohen, 1990).

Legislation and government guidance recognises the importance of young people's mental health; specifically, there have been developments from a national policy context of legislation within education and health to promote mental and emotional health and wellbeing (Scottish Executive, 2005a). The Education (Additional Support for Learning) (Scotland) Act 2004 states that education authorities must make provision for children and young people's additional support needs; the assessment for additional support includes psychological needs. How then do we meet these psychological needs? We must turn to the profile of abilities and adapt our remedial strategies of support to compensate for these more subtle and less understood needs.

A further document produced by the Scottish Executive entitled 'The Mental Health of Children and Young People: A Framework for Promotion, Prevention and Care' (Scottish Executive, 2005b) outlined a commitment to ensure that every child has the best possible start in life and is able to reach their full potential. This framework promoted by Scottish Ministers contained the expectation that children and young people in Scotland should be valued by ensuring that they are:

1. Safe:

Children and young people should be protected from abuse, neglect and harm by others at home, at school and in the community. As with the general population people on the autism spectrum are not immune from the aspects of abuse and neglect mentioned above. However, if we look at the profile of abilities, specifically the area of vulnerability, this may possibly predispose individuals with autism to situations opposed to positive mental health. Taking an aspect of mental wellbeing such as self-esteem and using the definition "An evaluation of personal worth based on the difference between one's ideal-self and one's self-concept" (Humphrey 2004), we can see that if individual wellbeing for people with ASD is going to be secured in an inclusive society, appropriate adaptations that recognise and meet their profile of abilities need to be made.

Case example taken from a teenager (15 year old female) with Asperger's Syndrome:

"What's self-esteem? ... [after an explanation] ... I have very low self-esteem. I've been bullied so much I'm too anxious to go to school. I have really high anxiety and I can't go out."

(Robinson, 2007)

2. Nurtured:

Children and young people should live within a supportive family setting, with additional assistance if required, or, where this is not possible, within another caring setting, ensuring a positive and rewarding childhood experience.

The key element of this point refers to 'additional assistance if required'. People with an ASD by the very nature of their condition may require specially adapted assistance to meet their social and emotional needs as well as differences in ways of learning.

3. **Healthy:**

   Children and young people should enjoy the highest attainable standards of physical and mental health, with access to suitable healthcare and support for safe and healthy lifestyle choices.

Focus should be given to the point referring to 'safe and healthy lifestyle choices' as these may be abstract concepts requiring concrete teaching, plus recognition should be given to the fact that there are some people with an ASD that find real informed choice difficult.

4. **Achieving:**

   Children and young people should have access to positive learning environments and opportunities to develop their skills, confidence and self esteem to the fullest potential.

5. **Active:**

   Children and young people should be active with opportunities and encouragement to participate in play and recreation, including sport.

As has previously been outlined the learning requirements of those with an ASD require adaptation to meet the profile of abilities. Adaptive supports to meet the difficulties experienced with imaginative thought and social play are required. Others can be a source of confusion; recreation might not follow the same patterns of interactive engagement and competitive sports might place the child in a vulnerable position, due to rigid rule application or a lack of internal motivation to 'beat' the other team.

6. **Respected and responsible:**

   Children, young people and their carers should be involved in decisions that affect them, should have their voices heard and should be encouraged to play an active and responsible role in their communities.

Encouraging participant involvement requires that the person possesses awareness that one has a choice and the ability to self-advocate; both of these issues that require adaptation in order for young people's views to be heard.

7. **Included:**

   Children, young people and their carers should have access to high quality services, when required, and should be assisted to overcome the social, educational, physical, environmental and economic barriers that create inequality.

- *This commitment outlined by the Scottish Executive is to ensure that each child and young person has the best possible start in life and is able to reach their full potential. This should coincide with consideration and appropriate adaptations to meet the profile of abilities present for those with an ASD. It is the careful consideration with adaptation to meet the differing needs that supports the commitment of each child with an ASD in meeting their potential.*

Furthermore, as previously stated, the then Scottish Executive recognised that the transition into secondary school, 'is marked by increased exposure to risks that may predispose young people to poor mental health … [including the] onset of anxiety, depression, eating disorders, substance misuse, psychosis and deliberate self-harm'. The profile of abilities faced by those with an ASD exacerbates the impact of personal, micro and macro transitions. In an attempt to address the needs arising from this stress invoking period the Executive proposed the following:

- Developing and building the emotional literacy of our children and young people and supporting them through the many transitions they face.
- Continue to develop and expand school-based programmes on positive emotional mental health and well-being.

In order to appreciate emotional literacy one should first turn to the concept of emotional intelligence. 'Emotional Intelligence' has been defined as:

- *'A form of social intelligence that involves the ability to monitor one's own and others' feelings and emotions, to discriminate among them, and to use this information to guide one's thinking and action.'*

Salovey and Mayer (1990)

The concept of 'emotional literacy' (EL) is derived largely from academic psychological work on emotional intelligence that has emerged and developed largely outside of the academic and policy mainstream (Sutton, Love, Bell, Christie, Mayrhofer, Millman, Williams and Yuill, 2005). It has been defined as:

- *'The ability to recognise, understand, handle and appropriately express emotions.'*

(Southampton Emotional Literacy Interest Group, 1998 cited by Sutton et al, 2005)

Emotional literacy has developed from the academic work on emotional intelligence together with educational programmes devised in the USA covering 'social and emotional learning' (SEL). The aim of emotional literacy is to develop the emotional competence of children and young people. Whereas the context of emotional literacy is primarily targeted at schools perhaps because educators are familiar with the concept of 'literacy' and it is therefore is a more familiar concept for teachers (Weare, 2004).

From the grid on the next page the need to concretely address the area of emotional literacy for those with an ASD is fairly apparent. However, it must be stressed that this is a particular area of impairment that requires adaptation. It is recommended that when engaging children and young people in social and emotional learning that you target their strengths. Many pupils with ASD particularly those with Asperger's Syndrome will be academically able and often excel in areas of personal interest. In contrast to this their emotional intelligence may well be functioning at a developmentally lower age. It has been proposed that for those with Asperger's Syndrome emotional maturity is usually three years behind peers (Attwood, 2007), this coupled with a limited vocabulary to describe emotions is a strong argument for targeting emotional intelligence. However, making things meaningful and not purely an academic exercise is pivotal to this area of development. Although teaching in emotional understanding and emotional literacy is fundamental using their academic ability as a positive gauge can act as a preventative measure to perhaps having a negative impact on their self-esteem.

2.8.5 The Impact of ASD on Emotional Well-being (Grid 9)

The Impact of ASD on Emotional Well-being	
Impact of ASD	**Responding to the needs of pupils with ASD**
Links to HGIOS Quality Indicators (highlighted by theme)	
1.1 Improvement in performance *Themes:* • Standards of attainment over time • Overall quality of learners' achievement • Impact of the school improvement plan 2.1 Learners' experiences *Themes:* • The extent to which learners are motivated and actively involved in their own learning and development 5.1 The curriculum *Themes:* • Programmes and courses • Transitions 5.2 Teaching for effective learning *Themes:* • The learning climate and teaching approaches • Teacher-pupil interaction including learners' engagement • Clarity and purposefulness of dialogue	5.3 Meeting learning needs *Themes:* • Tasks, activities and resources • Identification of learning needs 5.4 Assessment for learning *Themes:* Planning learning experiences and activities 5.5 Expectations and promoting achievement *Themes:* • Learner expectations and sense of achievement • Promoting and sustaining an ethos of achievement 5.6 Equality and Fairness *Themes:* • Approaches to inclusion • Promoting equality and fairness • Ensuring equality and fairness 5.8 Care, welfare and development *Themes:* • Approaches to and provision for meeting the emotional, physical and social needs of children and young people
Refer to HMIE *Education for Pupils with Autism Spectrum Disorder* Recommendations 2, 3, 4 and 8	

The Impact of ASD on Emotional Well-being	
Impact of ASD	**Responding to the needs of pupils with ASD**
• The pupil with ASD may possess a scattered profile of abilities however the core areas of difficulty being primarily in social communication, social interaction, play, imagination and flexible thinking mean that they may be less likely to engage in shared experiences. This may impact on their motivation to join in group activities, such as social games and sports.	• Present structured opportunities for group interaction within the school day. Use information gathered from baseline assessments of their profile of abilities. Prepare the pupil for group interaction through visually timetabled information of when and for how long group interaction sessions will take place. Develop visual materials to support their expected involvement and incorporate the involvement of others within the interactions.

The Impact of ASD on Emotional Well-being	
Impact of ASD	**Responding to the needs of pupils with ASD**
• Misunderstandings may arise due to the pragmatics of language, interpersonal engagement (they may misinterpret the unspoken meanings within the interaction).	• Provide written information (if at their cognitive level) of the rationale for participating in such an activity. This information should attempt to address such issues as difficulties with theory of mind (others perspective) and difficulties with central coherence (getting the social meaning).
• A lack of understanding of social interaction skills and missing the social context of situations often leaves the pupil with ASD on the periphery and often isolated.	• Accept that there may be areas of 'blindness' within the social interplay that they not be able to achieve naturally or through adaptations.
• The pupil with ASD may possess difficulties with a range of emotional management skills. There may be little awareness of internal states such as feelings of anxiety, anger or sadness. Due to the high social demands of school pupils are often experiencing high levels of anxiety or stress. Emotional awareness may not occur until the pupil loses control in an outburst that may appear to others as coming from nowhere. Difficulties processing others perspectives, a lack of awareness of others emotional states and a limited ability to emotionally match others moods are all indicative of a lack of emotional understanding.	• Use pupil's interest to aid success within the group activity. This can then be used as a concrete experience and a reference point to encourage further involvement within other less favoured group activities.
• Understanding self-awareness may require focused teaching. Specialist approaches to teaching understanding of their own condition may be required. They may develop more awareness of their differences within a mainstream peer group.	• Develop a visual emotional understanding programme (there are a range of resources that attempt to support this, see the resource section).

The Impact of ASD on Emotional Well-being	
Impact of ASD	**Responding to the needs of pupils with ASD**
• Difficulties building positive self-esteem. • Rigidity of thought and need for sameness may result with difficulties arsing from difficulties with executive functioning.	• Teach the associations of feelings with experience. This requires immediate association, therefore, when they show behaviours that indicate a feeling or state, teach this association immediately. Augment this learning by developing concrete visual supports (such as an 'emotions folder').
• Difficulties building emotional resilience. • A pupil may possess limited self-awareness and therefore may not be aware of internal feelings or mood states.	• Providing the person with ASD specific counselling if they reach a state of distress (remember it is essential that the person providing therapeutic counselling is aware of the profile of abilities). Counselling may be useful for more able pupils and should be accessed only of the young person wishes to access this type of therapeutic support.
• A 'fragile sense of self' may leave pupils vulnerable to additional mental health difficulties.	• Teach others to understand the pupils 'differences' by having awareness-raising sessions (this should only occur if the pupil and their parents have given their consent. Some pupils with Asperger's Syndrome are very private regarding disclosing their condition to others). • Help the person understand their condition and the impact this has. This can be done with specific resources - see 'I am Special' (Vermulen, 2001) (Section 6 - Resources, 65) or with specialist therapeutic group interventions (Video Interpersonal Self-Reflection Assessment Method (VIS-RAM, Robinson, 2005).

The Autism Toolbox

Part 2
Section 2.9

Transitions

2.9 Transitions

Transitions can be very problematic for pupils on the autistic spectrum due mainly to their cognitive processing of the environment and need for predictability. Children are likely to have difficulties with:

- Interpreting the thoughts/feelings/expectations of new people (Theory of Mind);
- Understanding or establishing appropriate new routines (weak Central Coherence);
- Planning and organisation (Executive Functioning);
- Sensory processing.

All of the above can provoke high levels of anxiety and may result in unusual behaviours or responses, such as:

- Fear;
- Inappropriate reactions due to lack of social understanding and what behaviour is expected;
- Attempts to keep environment the same, or negative responses to transition interfering with existing structures;
- Non compliance;
- Behaviour that adults find challenging.

Pupils need to know…

- Where they have to be
- Who might be there
- What they will/should be doing
- What behaviour is expected
- How much they have to do
- How they will they know they are finished
- What they will be doing next.

(Division TEACCH, 2006)

These points are not unreasonable: as adults we tend to expect children to do what they are told without question. However, if sent on a course or to a meeting most of us would be uncomfortable without at least the above information!

Types of transition

There are numerous types of transition that occur throughout the day, the school term, the year and across the lifespan. It is not always the major transitions that have the most impact on pupils on the spectrum but all need to be considered and planned for where possible. At the very least, coping with transition needs to be recognised as a potential stressor for pupils and their families. The following are a selection of common transitions:

- From one educational placement to another (new building, new people, new structures etc.).
- From stage to stage
- Different areas of the school
- Home to school
- Different/new personnel
- Home issues (new house/new baby/bereavement/holidays)
- Personal transitions as a result of maturation and development

Preparing a pupil on the autistic spectrum for a transition can vary widely, such as a trusted adult taking five minutes to explain why there has been change to the day, going to the assembly hall early to rehearse where you will sit before the hall is too busy, or a large multi-disciplinary team preparing a child to move between educational establishments. Whatever the scale or complexity of the transition the most important factor is to consider the situation from the perspective of the pupil, taking account of their strengths, difficulties and past experiences.

The following issues need to be considered when planning transitions between key stages. Some will also be appropriate for the day-to-day transitions.

Pupil preparation

- Explore classroom and unfamiliar areas of school:
    - Identify times when class is empty – break/Gym/drama
    - Emphasise function of areas and 'rules'
    - Photographs or video to discuss at home

- Activities in classroom as an individual:
    - Transfer visuals where appropriate
    - Discuss and model 'how to.... In P1'
    - Identify key resources and practise key procedures (cloakroom/register/lunches etc.)

- Introduce key staff in familiar environment before meeting them in new environment
- Activities in new environment as part of small group led by familiar adult
- Where appropriate, discuss differences between familiar and new environments
    - Unfamiliar vocabulary
    - Timetables and subjects
    - Equipment needed/organisation
- Identify Buddy/monitor/prefect/key adults
- Provide factual information about school and staff - it may seem irrelevant but can be important and reassuring to pupils on the autistic spectrum. School handbooks and websites can be particularly useful
- Problem solving using school scenarios, focusing on locating appropriate individuals to help if things go wrong and keeping safe (see Resource 26)
- Individual concerns
- It is important to be flexible and understanding. However, it is equally important to be clear about expectations from the start

Staff preparation

The emphasis tends to be on individual pupils and their difficulties. However, it is equally and in fact, often more important to prepare staff who will be working with the pupil. The following should be considered:

- Whole school in-service/development sessions (Ideally delivered jointly with other services)
- Personal experience and concerns/fears
- Distribution of current pupil profiles, pen portraits, or home information
- Collaboration time for staff to transfer information
- Informal meeting with parents
- Consultation with support services
- Advice regarding classroom layout, current strategies, IEP targets
- Multi-professional transition meeting
- On-going support from senior management and appropriate agencies
- Access to autism specific courses

Parental Concerns

Major transitions between stages are stressful for most parents; if their children have ASN/ASD they cannot take the most basic elements of the transition for granted. In some cases they may have had a negative experience and be particularly anxious that mistakes are not repeated or that professionals are taking their concerns seriously. It is not suggested that schools do everything parents ask, but there must be a dialogue. Parent - school relationships are one of the most influential factors in successful placements.

It can be immensely beneficial if schools are pro-active in collating and valuing information from the home environment, even if it is only to make staff aware that a pupil is not sleeping and may be less tolerant than usual. Best practice occurs when schools work with parents to address home issues as well as school issues when appropriate. The following are common issues for parents:

- Safety
- Toileting
- Behaviours
- Child's communication
- Other children
- Siblings
- Homework
- Eating
- Sleeping
- Parents' role
- Communication with Staff
- Curriculum
- If things go wrong...

A transition plan should be prepared reflecting the individual circumstances of each transition and distributed to all concerned (examples 14 - p128, 15 - p128 and 16 - p129).

Example 14 - Nursery - Primary transition

Transition practices are often well developed for all children moving between nursery and primary education. Very young children often lack the capacity to generalise their experiences across settings and therefore nursery and primary staffs increasingly work together to develop shared practices and to ensure that the new primary classroom is familiar to school entrants. For the child with autism it is particularly important that the context allows them to make use of prior learning.

In the second year of nursery Ben often sought out Mark's company. The boys shared an interest in building Lego constructions for which Mark with his special interest in written words would write out labels. In the last term of nursery school their shared interests expanded into more social play with cars and with a wider range of construction materials. Ben led the way in social situations whilst Mark provided depth of knowledge on particular topics. Both were going on to the same primary school which had 2 primary 1 classes. It had been decided to split the intake by age – the boys were 4 months apart and Mark was allocated to the older group where it was felt his academic skills were more likely to be matched by those of other children. However Mark knew few of the children entering his new class. His nursery teacher suggested it would be important for Mark to go to school with his friend, Ben, who quite naturally provided him with necessary social support and could read the social situation and social interactions readily.

At first the primary staff were reluctant to make this exception to intake plans, but after seeing how isolated Mark was on his induction days, and how anxious he became, the primary 1 teachers arranged to observe in the nursery school, and agreed that it was in Mark's best interests to go to school with his friend. The nursery teacher worked with the 2 boys to produce a book showing some of their Lego designs, annotated by Mark – this was added to the primary 1 class library before the boys left nursery.

Example 15 - Primary - Secondary transition

An 11 year old boy leaving a base for pupils on the autism spectrum and moving to a base within a high school. With help from a speech and language therapist, the pupil made up a communication passport to take with him to his new school. The pupil was asked what he would like people to know about him. He came up with several suggestions i.e. about his family, who his friends are, special things and people to him, places that he likes to go, how can others help him communicate, when he might need help, how to help him, what to do if he gets upset and things that he did not like doing. After discussions with the pupil it was felt that he should inform people in his passport that he has an autism spectrum disorder. The new school found this document to be invaluable.

A circle of friend with 8 pupils who would be attending the same high school was set up to support the pupil in getting to know his peers on a more social level. They had lunch together once a

continued on next page

week for 6 months leading up to High School. His class teacher visited his new school with his parents before they decided on his placement. After the placement was confirmed his class teacher arranged for the High School staff to visit the Primary School environment. The following week the pupil visited the High School and looked around. This was an opportunity to take photos of the pupil in every class along with the staff that he would be working with. The pupil made a power point presentation of his new classes. He visited the High School with his SLA to again familiarise himself with the surroundings. The pupil participated in two moving up days unsupported by his primary school. He thoroughly enjoyed them and felt comfortable in his new surroundings.

Example 16 - Making a successful transition to University

1) Early communication between applicant and key university staff

In some cases, this communication, when instigated by the applicant, their family or school, can start as early as a year prior to entry; generally speaking, the earlier the better. It allows opportunities to plan for transition, to allow the applicant to build relations with key university staff – in both their academic department and the Disability Service – and to start familiarisation with the University/campus environment. Where students will require adjustments to assessment (such as extra time in written exams) or may require additional support (such as equipment or a Mentor), diagnostic evidence is typically required. It is helpful if the school can make available any relevant information regarding the applicant's diagnosis, the impact of their difficulties and the nature of any support provided at school.

2) Opportunities to experience University prior to start of course

Some applicants will make use of structured opportunities to 'try out' University by participating in the GOALS project or by attending the Summer School. A range of opportunities are appropriate, and Strathclyde University also includes participation in the Summer Transition Programme (run by the Disability Service in collaboration with the National Autistic Society) and the Effective Learning Programme (a series of small group study skills sessions offered to all disabled applicants and students). Open days offer another opportunity to visit academic departments and become familiar with the University environment.

3) Engaging with relevant external agencies

Both the Disability Service and an increasing number of academic departments will have valuable experience of supporting previous applicants/students with AS. However, the breadth and depth of experience and expertise – such as offered by NAS - is a valuable source of support to both Universities and the applicant and their family. NAS will offer applicants and their families more general support with preparation for University including assistance with form filling and liaising with the University.

continued on next page

4) Supported transition

Having additional one-to-one support at key stages in the transition can make a huge difference. A Mentor can accompany and/or guide a new student through the bewildering procedures surrounding registration, signing up for tutorial groups, finding teaching classrooms, locating the toilets, cafes and quiet spaces, attending events in Freshers' Week, joining the gym or special interest clubs and societies, using the library, getting on-line and so on. Some students will also benefit from one-to-one support from a Study Support Assistant (who might also be their Mentor), with organising their timetable, planning for deadlines, exploring strategies for note-taking and organising information and so on.

Having one-to-one support means the applicant or student has a 'trouble-shooter' to identify and address any potential difficulties or confusion on the spot.

2.9.1 The Impact of ASD on Transitions (Grid 10)

<table>
<tr><th colspan="2">The impact of ASD on Transitions</th></tr>
<tr><th>Impact of ASD</th><th>Responding to the needs of pupils with ASD</th></tr>
<tr><th colspan="2">Links to HGIOS Quality Indicators</th></tr>
<tr><td>1.2 Fulfilment of statutory duties
2.1 Learners' experiences
2.2 The school's success in involving parents, carers and families
4.1 The school's success in working with and engaging with the local community
4.2 The school's success in working with the wider community
5.1 The Curriculum
5.3 Meeting learning needs
5.4 Assessment for learning
5.5 Expectations and promoting achievement
5.6 Equality and fairness</td><td>5.7 Partnership with learners and parents
5.8 Care, welfare and development
7.2 Staff deployment and teamwork
7.3 Staff development and review
8.1 Partnerships with the community, educational establishments, agencies and employers
8.3 Management and use of resources and space for learning
8.4 Managing information
9.1 Vision, values and aims
9.2 Leadership and direction
9.3 Developing people and partnerships</td></tr>
<tr><td colspan="2">Refer to HMIE Education for Pupils with Autism Spectrum Disorder Recommendations 3, 4, 5, 7 and 8</td></tr>
</table>

<table>
<tr><th colspan="2">The impact of ASD on Transitions</th></tr>
<tr><th>Impact of ASD</th><th>Responding to the needs of pupils with ASD</th></tr>
<tr><td>• Resistance to change with a preference for the familiar, is a key feature of individuals on the spectrum. Transition of any kind is likely to involve elements that are new whether that be people, expectations or contexts. Cognitive styles will influence individual interpretation, processing and understanding of new environments.</td><td>• Assessment to work towards an individualised transition plan should take place. This should take account of:
  • The pupil's capacity to cope with change
  • Key people or agencies who may be contributing to the transitions process.
  • Preparation visits.
  • Communication of information in a form that is accessible to the pupil.
  • Parental concerns.
  • CPD for staff.
  • Time (staff) – for planning, familiarisation and a reasonable timescale for the transition to take place.</td></tr>
</table>

The impact of ASD on Transitions	
Impact of ASD	**Responding to the needs of pupils with ASD**
	• Time (pupils) – to raise awareness of new processes vocabulary and get to know key staff. To explore new environments. To have an opportunity to share any concerns; • If appropriate formal and informal risk assessments may need to be incorporated in keeping with local policy guidance.
• Sensory processing difficulties may be heightened in new environments. Filtering of sensory information may be problematic and may result in stress reactions or increased anxiety leading to challenging or bizarre/inappropriate behaviours.	• During familiarisation visits staff should observe and take account of any adverse responses to environmental stimuli such as sounds, crowded areas, lighting, temperature or the proximity of others. • Measures may need to be taken to make reasonable adaptations to the environment. Expectations of what will be required of the pupil in particular settings may also need review and adjustment according to needs.
• The anticipation of transitions can be anxiety provoking. Events/transitions that are often welcomed and hoped for in typically developing pupils may be a source of fear and anxiety to pupils on the spectrum as they are unlikely to be able to assimilate an internal image of what the process may involve or what may occur in a new situation. They may also be unable to draw on similar, previous experiences in order to anticipate what may be involved or what may be required of them.	• It will also be important to identify areas where the pupil is comfortable as this may be a location they may use if they are stressed and need to take some time out. • These aspects should be considered as part of the initial assessment of the pupil. Additionally the views of the pupil and their parents/carers and previous teachers will be informative in developing approaches.

The impact of ASD on Transitions	
Impact of ASD	**Responding to the needs of pupils with ASD**
• Adjusting to the expectations of new sets of people in a new context is likely to be challenging and altering social behaviour in keeping with a changing context can be difficult for pupils with ASD.	• Connections between past and current experiences may not be immediately obvious to the pupil. Staff can draw on previous information to support the pupil to make connections and to offer reassurance. • The social rules and expectations of any situation need to be made explicit to pupils with ASD. Information needs to be presented in a way that meets their needs and may need to be continually accessible so that pupils can have a point of reference if they are unsure about expectations. Similarly such a point of reference will aid teachers in reminding pupils of behavioural expectations. • Visual information (e.g. photographs) or school websites will provide pupils with a concrete point of reference regarding new adults or the roles of adults in a new context.
• Given the complex and diverse nature of the needs of some individuals on the spectrum there are likely to be a variety of professionals involved. The pupil or parents may not fully understand their role or their involvement and may have only occasional contact with some of the involved professionals.	• The validity of time for involved professionals to communicate needs to be recognised. • Effective communication and shared perspectives between schools regarding supporting the transition of pupils with ASD is likely to lead to more proactive planning and supportive practice. • There is likely to be a role for senior management within schools to take responsibility for co-ordinating professional involvement when a range of agencies are represented. • Systems and approaches may need to be adapted so that pupils can engage in review processes. This may include the use of visual communication materials e.g. talking mats or time with a familiar supportive adult to prepare for review or other meetings. Visual rating scales may also be helpful.

The impact of ASD on Transitions	
Impact of ASD	**Responding to the needs of pupils with ASD**
• The potentially complex nature of ASD may give rise to concerns among staff. Such concerns may be due to incomplete records or misinformation about the nature of ASD in general and how it is impacting on the individual pupil in particular.	• Recording systems may need to be adapted to take account of the specific aspects that will be relevant for pupils with ASD. • Opportunities should be sought for formal and informal CPD to support staff who may feel anxious about their level of expertise in ASD. e.g. attendance at training courses, visiting ASD bases, networking with other agencies and schools, sharing good practice and building relationships with parents. Time to collate reading and other resources that will increase understanding and confidence. • On-going support from senior management. • Assessment of the individual pupil and circumstances as well as liaison between existing and future staff will be needed to ascertain the most appropriate time line.
• The lead in time for transitions to occur will be predicated by the individual impact of ASD on the pupil. Key elements are the capacity to appreciate the concept of the passage of time and their ability to cope with future, stressful events.	• The adults can begin the process well ahead of time even if the pupil will not be directly involved till a later stage. It is more effective to begin early and have time for a full analysis of the situation than to cause stress and risk failure by delaying.

2.9.2 Developmental Impact on Personal Transitions

'From the second year of life we find already the characteristic features that remain unmistakeable and constant throughout the whole life-span...'

(Asperger, 1944/1991, p.67)

The development of all children with ASD will be uneven and idiosyncratic, having a dramatic and often unexpected impact on personal transitions throughout the lifespan. In particular, areas of social communication, social interaction and flexibility of thought/social imagination will suffer significant delay. Furthermore,

'each impairment interacts with every other, so that they overflow and pervade each other; it is the interaction between different parts of the syndrome which is most characteristic of autism'.

(Newson cited by Jordan, 1999. Resource 21)

In accordance with a profile of uneven development, however, certain areas will be less affected. For example, fine/gross motor skills may be relatively intact (although these, too, can be affected in children with a diagnosis of Asperger's Syndrome (AS), or cognitive performance may be on a par with, or even above, that of their peers. Unfortunately the core areas of impairment will also impact on such relatively intact areas of development (e.g. a fundamental impairment in understanding communication will affect the understanding of a lesson when delivered verbally, despite the child having average intelligence).

Global learning disability if present will also impact on development across the board; however the key areas of impairment will be more greatly affected. Furthermore, the child may have other disorder/s affecting their development. The impact of each will need to be gauged and appropriately supported.

Another factor potentially impacting on personal transitions is that onset of epilepsy may occur at an increased rate and at an older age in children with autism as opposed to the general population: it is prevalent in a quarter to a third of children who have learning disability as well as autism, with onset most likely in the early teenage years (Ives and Munro, 2002) (Resource 61).

The uneven developmental profile characteristic of autism may result in other people having an unrealistic perception of the child's abilities and challenges throughout their life. This can work both ways, with areas of deficit perhaps masking peak skills, or apparent skill areas masking underlying impairment. While development and progress is expected, especially in children less severely affected by their ASD, if appropriately supported (Ives and Munro, 2002); unless their developmental profile is understood then teaching and intervention strategies are unlikely to be appropriately pitched.

As a result of such developmental challenges, the child will mature at a different rate to their peers with uneven/qualitatively different levels of maturation across different areas. An understanding of their developmental profile can be gained through assessment tools such as the Psychoeducational Profile-Revised (PEP-R. Schopler Reichler, Bashford et al, 1990) and its successor, the Psychoeducational Profile: Third Edition (PEP3. Schopler Lansing, Reichler and Marcus, 2005) (Resource 39). Across the board, the child's autism, and its interaction with other aspects of their profile, will impact on personal transitions, making them qualitatively different, and often delayed in relation to, those of their peers. The following will look at the potential impact of ASD at different stages of childhood below:

2.9.3 Early Childhood

Beginning with the pre-schooler, while physical development may have occurred in line with peers, or slightly slower, delays and differences will become increasingly apparent in social skills; communication; cognitive and self help skills.

When supporting a child with an ASD it is essential to keep in mind the framework of typical development. This constant reference to typical development provides insight into the actual achieved stages of development or developmental functioning for each child. Socially, the child may remain at the developmental level of 'parallel play' or not even reach this level, remaining aloof and alone. Interaction with others may be solely in order to have needs met (i.e. using others as tools), otherwise appearing passively indifferent to others. Alternatively, lack of understanding of social rules such as give and take may lead to a lack of reciprocal interaction seeing the child dominating play with other children.

Early communicative skills such as eye contact, sharing attention, pointing and joint attention are significantly affected, affecting subsequent development in not only communication, but areas such as imagination, social understanding and self help, too. Over 50% of all children with autism will not have developed speech by four years, and are unlikely to develop compensatory strategies, such as gesturing. Only about 25% of four year olds with autism have some meaningful speech, and this is likely to be extremely limited. The remaining 25% develop some speech but use it in a rote, echolalic fashion (repeating without meaning) (Harris, 2000). Use and understanding of non verbal communication is also likely to be affected, regardless of ability.

Play is likely to have a rigid, repetitive, non-social quality and, without focused intervention, probably not progress beyond the levels of *'sensori-motor' play* (involving sensory exploration of items, as seen in 6-8 month old babies); *'organizing play'* (where items are lined up or stacked with no understanding of their actual function – occurring at 6-9 months typical development) or limited *'functional play'* (using play objects according to function, as seen at age 9-12 months typical development) (Beyer and Gammeltoft, 1999) (*Resource 18*). This will be in stark contrast to peers, who at this age will be forming friendships and engaging in increasingly sophisticated imaginative and joint play.

At around 4 years, typically developing children will understand that other people think differently to them ('theory of mind'). This has a huge impact on their social understanding and interactions, however the child with autism is highly unlikely to make this developmental stage, leaving them vulnerable to others and unable to understand, communicate and interact in the same way as their peers.

In personal transitions to the acquisition of self help skills, milestones such as toilet training are likely to be delayed: almost half all children with autism are not toilet trained by the age of 4 (Powers, 2000) (*Resource 62*). Similarly, feeding and sleep difficulties may persist into later childhood and perhaps beyond. Changes to routine are likely to be extremely upsetting.

Difficulties in the above areas can lead to behavioural expression (Stoddart, 2004) (*Resource 23*) and tantrums may continue well beyond the expected age: 'Even for the most able, their attentional and emotional control may be below the level of a nine-month-old and so the behaviour shown is at a similar level' (Jordan, 2002) (*Resource 22*). Where appropriate, behaviour management programmes, based on an understanding of how autism impacts on the behaviour, should be implemented early on. Such intervention is likely to have a big impact on the likelihood of difficult behaviours such as aggression and self-injury continuing into adolescence (Powers, 2000).

Not only may the child with autism develop at a *slower rate* to their peers, but developmental milestones may occur in a *different sequence* to that expected (Powers, 2000). This again can add confusion as to actual developmental level. In some children of higher ability, difficulties may not be fully recognised, understood for what they are and accurately identified. This is usually due to the uneven developmental profile masking some areas of impairment (e.g. *surface* language ability deflecting from the *underlying* difficulties in social communication).

Early intervention (based on a thorough understanding of autism, and of the individual child's profile) is recognised as extremely important in supporting development (Stoddart, 2004; Jordan, 2002). Where this has not occurred, perhaps due to late diagnosis, developing an accurate understanding of the child in the context of their autism should enable appropriate intervention. It is important to view their difficulties from a developmental perspective and this may entail teaching very early social behaviours such as those seen in very young babies, despite their being at a much later chronological age, in an attempt to develop fundamental but missing skills. Practitioners should be aware of the many claims of success made by advocates of specific early intervention methods, and take a balanced view of these, informed by the research literature (Jordan, 2002).

In summary, whereas the typically developing child generally develops and flourishes socially, emotionally, cognitively and physically, smoothly transitioning through their developmental milestones, the child with autism is likely to move very slowly through many important personal transitions. This slow progress will undoubtedly impact on transition through later childhood and adolescent years.

2.9.4 Mid Childhood

As social behaviour amongst typical children becomes increasingly complex and sophisticated, that of the child with autism appears increasingly incongruous (Williams and Wright, 2004) (*Resource 31*). In higher functioning children, where earlier social difficulties may have been masked, the differences are now apparent: they are unlikely to have close friendships and important social behaviours such as sharing, losing gracefully and turn taking have not developed. Not picking up on unspoken social rules (e.g. 'not telling on' your class mates) may lead to avoidance, stigmatisation and bullying by other children. Behaviour towards adults is also likely to have an unusual quality.

Daily transitions such as school – home; break time and between subjects are likely to cause stress and anxiety disproportionate to that of peers. The impact of lacking certain early developmental skills will continue to manifest in areas such as difficulty learning through imitation.

Personal interests are likely to be out of line with those of their peers, due to content or intensity (e.g. talking volubly about train engines; trying to collect desk fans). The child will have difficulty sharing others' interests, perhaps leading to perceptions of being self centred. Sense of humour is likely to remain at a very concrete level (e.g. slapstick).

In children with AS, especially, there is an increased rate of mood disorders such as anxiety or depression occurring. These may require specialist/medical intervention (Attwood, 2007) (*Resource 60*) and are usually a result of their ongoing difficulties with socialising; coping with change; coping with sensory sensitivities and having to work that much harder than others in order to process and understand what is going on around them.

2.9.5 Adolescence

Again, if we look at typical development, the onset of adolescence brings with it a multitude of transitions, internal and external, leading to a 'more or less perpetual state of disequilibrium' (Boyd and Bee, 2003) (see also Boyd and Bee, 2008, *Resource 78*) and requiring development of new understandings and skills. While this is challenging enough for youngsters without autism, in many ways it can present even more of a challenge for this group. Furthermore, while the support of peers is central to this process in typical development, this mechanism is unlikely to be present, or indeed accessible by, the adolescent with autism. Puberty might also occur slightly later for some individuals with autism (Mortlock, 1993).

During early adolescence one's thinking moves from 'concrete operations' which are dependent on external objects and pictures to support concepts, to internalised 'formal, abstract operations' (Boyd and Bee, 2008). In autism however it is likely to remain at a concrete level, especially for those teenagers with additional intellectual impairment (Mortlock, 1993). Areas such as self awareness, abstract thinking, moral reasoning and manipulation of ideas will all be affected by the individual's autism. Changing their own behaviour and self perception in line with other people's new perceptions of them as young adults is another hurdle that will require emotional support and practical strategies. The physical changes of puberty too can cause considerable anxiety (e.g. refusal to accept new, larger clothing; shaving off bodily hair as it appears).

It should be pointed out that adolescence in autism may however bring increased flexibility and reduced behavioural problems. IQ is likely to remain stable; however an increase or decrease may sometimes occur. Improvement in flexibility, tolerance of change and social interest may also occur. Some factors which suggest a more positive long term outcome for the child are level of cognitive ability; development of some spontaneous speech by age five or six and 'systematic early intervention'. However, the difficulties stemming from the triad of impairments will still pervade and for some the symptoms of autism may increase in severity (Powers, 2000).

The higher functioning teen with ASD may be aware of their developmental differences and the difficulties these cause, perhaps leading to secondary mental health problems. For example, they may be aware that peers are developing opposite sex relationships, but are themselves unsuccessful at this, lacking the skills and understanding required (Stoddart, 2004). It may be that a developmental crisis, in which the teenager is unable to meet key targets reached by his or her peers, is the start of the actual process of receiving a diagnosis of AS in a teenager hitherto undiagnosed (Atwood, 2007). Individuals with learning disability as well as autism may actually be protected by their disability from this acute insight into their difficulties, however deterioration in mental well being in adolescence has been found in 10% of people with autism (Rutter, 1970, cited Mortlock, 1993).

The transition from primary to secondary school can be an extremely difficult process. Not only is the environment and peer group changing, but also daily routines; expectations of others; range of teachers and classrooms; teaching styles; unstructured break times; increased workload; the need to increasingly organise themselves and their own learning, and physical development. The interests and social behaviour of typical peers will also be changing dramatically but unlikely to be shared or understood by the adolescent with autism. Hormonal changes will create further difficulties, the nature of which may be hard for the adolescent to understand. The above will all be compounded by difficulties created by the autism such as understanding changes going on around/inside them; interpreting and expressing their difficulties in a way that others understand; and seeking and receiving social support.

Finally, the major transition into adulthood will be looming as the young person approaches school leaving age. The direct impact of this transition will vary from person to person, however, given their autism, it can be expected that they will require considerable support both to understand and to undertake such transition. While peers will be striving for independence and considering concepts such as future career and personal aspirations, those with autism are likely to need planned and sustained support to think futuristically and to work towards the achievement of goals and ambitions.

2.9.6 The Impact of ASD on Personal Transitions (Grid 11)

The impact of ASD on Personal Transitions	
Impact of ASD	**Responding to the needs of pupils with ASD**
Links to HGIOS Quality Indicators (highlighted by theme)	
Quality Indicator: Key performance outcomes: 1.1 Improvement in performance *Themes:* • Standards of attainment over time • Overall quality of learners' achievement 2.1 Impact on learners: Learners' experiences *Themes:* • The extent to which learners are motivated and actively involved in their own learning and development • Delivery of education **Quality Indicator: Delivery of education:** 5.1 The curriculum *Themes:* • Programmes and courses • Transitions 5.2 Teaching for effective learning *Themes:* • The learning climate and teaching approaches • Teacher-pupil interaction including learners' engagement • Clarity and purposefulness of dialogue • Judgments made in the course of teaching	• Tasks, activities and resources • Identification of learning needs 5.4 Assessment for learning *Themes:* • Planning learning experiences and activities 5.5 Expectations and promoting achievement *Themes:* • Learner expectations and sense of achievement • Promoting and sustaining an ethos of achievement 5.6 Equality and fairness Themes: • Approaches to inclusion • Promoting equality and fairness • Ensuring equality and fairness 5.8 Care, welfare and development *Themes*: • Approaches to and provision for meeting the emotional, physical and social needs of children and young people • Delivery of education
Refer to HMIE *Education for Pupils with Autism Spectrum Disorder* Recommendations 3, 4, 5 and 8	

The impact of ASD on Personal Transitions	
Impact of ASD	**Responding to the needs of pupils with ASD**
• ASD is a developmental disorder and therefore developmental life transitions may be out of step with typical development. • As part of the developmental profile of abilities an ASD specific assessment can indicate in certain areas of functioning (for example imitation) a severe delay in development. • The impact of this developmental delay may result in the pupil with ASD being placed in an environment that they are not 'developmentally ready for' or have yet to acquire the skills to enable them to adapt, cope or even function adequately. This can translate into a conflict of expectations from parents and teaching staff.	• Bear in mind the scattered profile of abilities and how this can be associated with typical development. Using typical development as a guide provides insight into why the pupil behaves in certain ways based on their developmental functioning. Observations gained from assessing developmental functioning enables teachers to develop programmes targeting these levels thus providing greater scope for successful planning and intervention. • Assess individual skills separately (i.e. imitation skills, cognitive verbal performance, nonverbal communication etc) against typical development and focus interventions and teaching strategies accordingly. • ASD specific assessments are available (Pep3, AAPEP and TTAP, Section 6 – Resources 39, 52) and provide a developmental profile of skills. Knowledge of the pupil's developmental profile.
• For a pupil with an ASD typical adjustments to transitions may follow a different pattern to that of typically developing children. Transitions may be extended; elongated or delayed (an example of this may be seen through the pupil taking several months to adjust to the changing school year).	• There should be an expectation that pupils with an ASD plus additional learning disability will possess a range of skills significantly younger than their chronological age and their peer group.
• There may be a delay in the pupils capacity to deal with the impact of their own emotional states (an example may be that they do not respond to stereotyped messages, i.e. 'too big to cry').	• There should be an expectation that the child will not necessarily 'naturally' develop emotional management skills and these may need concrete teaching (this can be achieved through visual teaching, for example a 'feelings thermometer' or the 'angry volcano').

The impact of ASD on Personal Transitions	
Impact of ASD	**Responding to the needs of pupils with ASD**
• There may be a delay in achieving an appropriate level of behavioural responsibility (the ability to take on personal responsibility for ones own actions). • The pupil may be delayed in their development of acquiring personal responsibility skills in relation to self-help and personal care. • There may be a further delay in the pupil acquiring extended personal skills (for example they may not possess the skills of safety or organisational management that would enable them to complete home work or travel independently to and from school).	• The ability to self-advocate may be a delayed or underdeveloped skill and therefore providing structured opportunities with a focused agenda to achieve this may be beneficial for the pupil with an ASD. The development of self-advocacy forums (i.e. 'pupil forums') where initially the concept of 'self-advocacy' is taught with visual adaptations that assist the pupil to 'put their view forward'. It is worth bearing in mind that this concept may be interpreted rigidly and the pupil will need to also understand that there are times when they may self-advocate, but this does not necessarily mean they will automatically receive a positive response – think beyond the actual immediate teaching to the possible longer term impact of the child's ASD (look at all aspects of teaching new skills and think contingency plans!).
• Development of personal interests may be out of synch with their peer group (there is acceptance of young children watching, collecting and playing with fire engines, less tolerance, rejection and ridicule may be the experience for an adolescent following this interest). A pupil with ASD may appear to get stuck with a fascination or interest that is usually associated with a much younger child. • Transitions of loss and bereavement may be atypical and result in delayed, unconventional or no apparent response.	• Channel times for indulging in own specific interests if this may make the child susceptible to being bullied and teach similarly matched age appropriate alternatives (bear in mind that the social and developmental age may be significantly younger than their peer group). • Concretely teaching the concept of 'loss' is critical for all children, but particularly for the pupil with an ASD as this is an abstract concept that one achieves through experience. A useful concrete way of doing this may be through the concept of 'broken'. (an example is outlined here: Allow the child to experience the 'loss' of a broken toy, let the child see and hear your explanation of the toy being broken and then jointly dispose of the toy explaining that 'the toy is broken, so we throw it away and we wont see it again'). This may help to develop their understanding of loss and bereavement.

The impact of ASD on Personal Transitions	
Impact of ASD	**Responding to the needs of pupils with ASD**
• The impact of separation may be atypical (the pupil may not appear to respond to the separation of parents; they may appear to show signs of 'stranger anxiety' for an extended period of time). • There may be resistance to physical changes (i.e. voice breaking, secondary sexual characteristics).	• Concretely teaching the different aspects of separation may be necessary in an educational context as a means of teaching the pupil what separation and reunion can mean. When teaching concepts out of context (i.e. divorce) to pupils on the spectrum think of this teaching opportunity as a fundamental step to their 'social and life translation'. Facilitate the development of life dictionaries; social understanding (life concepts) 'portfolios' these can act as concrete reference points to aid their understanding of social situation either at the time or later on in their life if they experience such an event.

The Autism Toolbox

Part 2
Section 2.10

Whole School Approaches

2.10 Whole School Approaches

Pupils with autism are everyone's concern. Understanding of inclusion and inclusive practice is evolving. Whilst it is important to focus on individual needs and classroom practice, a whole school ethos and approach is needed to promote and sustain a culture of inclusiveness. The Centre for Inclusive Education suggests that "Inclusion happens when everyone feels appreciated and welcome to participate" (www.csie.org.uk). In essence this sounds quite straightforward. The challenge for head teachers, class teachers, support staff, pupils and parents is to ensure that such a culture permeates at all levels and in all activities and settings throughout the school.

It is important to consider some of the areas schools may need to focus on to ensure that approaches are indicative of inclusive education for pupils on the autism spectrum. These are likely to include:

- Playground issues
- Visually communicative environment
- Buddy or friendship support systems
- Safe havens
- Special interest lunch and after school clubs
- Promotion of positive perceptions of diversity
- Attitudes
- CPD for staff
- Auxiliary and support staff etc included in any awareness training
- Meaningful parental involvement supported by effective home/school communication
- Robust anti – bullying practices
- Recognition that bullying for children on spectrum may take many forms and indeed they may be easily led into being bullies themselves
- Count them in rather than leave them out attitude
- Willingness to take reasonable steps to adapt the environment
- Equity but individuality
- Recognising wider achievement

Ainscow (2008) suggests that "A detailed consideration of the barriers experienced by some pupils can help us to develop forms of schooling that will be more effective for all pupils" (www.csie.org.uk). It is therefore likely that investment in policy and practice that support and enhance the educational context for children on the spectrum will be of benefit to all and will contribute to the development of a more inclusive and thriving school community.

Example 17 - Whole school approaches/understanding

A pupil was successfully integrating into mainstream classes for gym, art, drama, music and RME. The next step was for this child was to have lunch in the main dining hall with her mainstream class then play with a group of her friends in the playground afterwards. Careful planning with the mainstream teacher and dining hall staff was then followed by training for the two children who had volunteered to be the pupil's buddies during this time. The pupil was then involved in planning. Base staff ensured that she had a clear understanding of the sequence of events that she would be involved in and the staff and children who would be able to help her should difficulties arise. The pupil now confidently integrates with her RME class and joins them in the dining hall and playground on a weekly basis without any support from the Base staff.

2.10.1 The Environment

Most practitioners would agree that the physical environment plays a significant role in the effective teaching and learning of most pupils. For pupils on the autism spectrum the impact of the environment is likely to need specific consideration. It is recognised that this is an under researched area however when the overall potential impact of the spectrum is considered the relevance of the environment becomes more apparent. Information processing, perception, cognition and sensory processing are all thought to be significant factors for pupils on the spectrum. All of these aspects will have an impact on how a child or young person interacts with and within a specific environment.

A key principle of inclusive practice is that adjustment should be made to enable the child to access the curriculum, school, home life and their community. The physical environment plays a critical role in this as does the culture and ethos of the school.

"Environmental supports are materials that assist the individual children, taking into account their sensory needs, their need to understand the passage of time, their modes of learning and strengths, and their need for accurate, reliable information."

(Dalrymple, 1995, 244)

Implementing the use of environmental supports need not be complex, they are in fact something most people rely on in new and familiar settings. A degree of individuality will be required however as stated in other sections such adjustments are essential for the child on the spectrum but beneficial to peers.

Evaluating the environment and taking account of potential impact will be important in relation to assessment. Secondary pupils taking award bearing exams may be significantly disadvantaged in certain environments. Jackson (2002) describes his dread of exams being taken in large halls due to being unable to bear the sound of everyone turning pages over. Whilst still poorly understood such sensory sensitivities are frequently reported by children and young people on the spectrum.

The National Autistic Society advocate the use of the SPELL framework (National Autistic Society, 2008). The acronym stands for:

Structure
Positive approaches
Empathy
Low Arousal
Links

Each area is related to a set of indicators and outcomes. The framework is based on the view that people with autism benefit from structure which helps them to anticipate routines of the day, from positive approaches which are based on respect and are put into place by practitioners who can empathise with how it is to be on the spectrum. Environments that are not over-stimulating are also believed to be helpful especially in relation to sensory issues. Finally SPELL recognises the need for working together in the interests of the person with ASD. Specific training in developing and applying the framework is available via the National Autistic Society.

Dalrymple (1995) offers a more individualised approach to evaluating the environment and suggests that for a pupil on the spectrum teachers will need to take account of a range of aspects including: communication; sensitivity to change; dependency on cues; awareness of time and the passing of time, and sensory needs.

It may be necessary to make adaptations to general areas of the school environment, or at least try to view them from the perspective of a child on the autistic spectrum, individual schools will vary, but common areas which can be challenging are:

- Playground
- Cafeteria
- Gym hall/assembly hall
- Computer suite
- Cloakrooms
- Structured play area
- Moving around school/corridors/between classrooms or buildings
- Arriving at or leaving school

When necessary it is just as important that there are clear structures and expectations. It is crucial, that all relevant staff are aware of the pupil's potential difficulties and agreed targets or strategies, including visual supports, to be implemented in these areas, e.g. catering and janitorial staff, office staff, support assistants, other teachers who do not work directly with the pupil.

These areas of school are generally unstructured and taking part in the playground or cafeteria, for example, will require a high level of interaction with peers and or adults, creating the most likely situation for things to break down for pupils on the autistic spectrum. Arrangements can be simple, such as:

- Allowing children to enter areas such as the cloakroom or lunch hall slightly early, before they become overwhelming.
- Allowing time to observe drama or gym activities before participating provides a mental model of what might be expected.
- Alternative supported activities at lunch time e.g. computer club can channel social activity, this can be especially helpful if there is a link to special interests.
- Rehearsing or practising moving around the school independently can minimise stress.

Some may have concerns about taking time away from formal curricular activities, however, if these areas of learning need are incorporated into Individualised Educational Programmes (IEPs) they open up learning and are legitimate and important activities to allow pupils to access their learning environment fully.

2.10.2 The Impact of ASD on Whole School Approaches (Grid 12)

The Impact of ASD on Whole School Approaches	
Impact of ASD	**Responding to the needs of pupils with ASD**
Links to HGIOS Quality Indicators	
1.1 Improvements in performance 1.2 Fulfilment of statutory duties 2.1 Learners' experiences 2.2 The school's success in involving parents, carers and families 3.1 The engagement of staff in the life and work of the school 4.1 The school's success in working with and engaging with the local community 4.2 Engaging with the wider community 5.2 Teaching for effective learning 5.3 Meeting learning needs 5.4 Assessment for learning 5.5 Expectations and promoting achievement	5.6 Equality and fairness 5.7 Partnership with learners and parents 5.8 Care, welfare and development 7.3 Staff development and review 8.1 Partnerships with the community, educational establishments, agencies and employers 8.2 Management of finance for learning 8.3 Management and use of resources and space for learning 8.4 Managing information 9.1 Vision, values and aims 9.2 Leadership and direction 9.4 Leadership of improvement and change
Refer to HMIE *Education for Pupils with Autism Spectrum Disorder* Recommendations 3, 4, 5, 6, 7, and 8	

The Impact of ASD on Whole School Approaches	
Impact of ASD	**Responding to the needs of pupils with ASD**
• Pupils with ASD may find the playground or breaks in the routine of school day quite threatening and anxiety provoking. Young children may find it difficult to participate in the games of other children particularly imaginative play. Older, secondary pupils may find it very difficult to "break in" to social groups and networks and may feel very isolated during unstructured times of the day.	• Buddy or friendship support systems are likely to be more appropriate for younger children and can form the basis of meaningful work in the area of citizenship. • Older pupils may need an identified safe haven within the school. This may be a room or indeed a trusted member of staff they can seek out when they are feeling stressed or overwhelmed.

The Impact of ASD on Whole School Approaches	
Impact of ASD	**Responding to the needs of pupils with ASD**
	• Many pupils on the spectrum have special interests. Lunch clubs and after school clubs based on such interests can promote the inclusion of pupils and also add to the community of the school. Special interests provide an excellent opportunity for pupils with ASD to shine. They will often have quite expert knowledge and this can help raise their self-esteem. Such expertise could also be utilised in guided study or homework clubs where they may be well placed to support younger or less able pupils.
• Pupils with ASD are unlikely to manage the school environment independently without a range of visual /verbal supports. ASD impacts on the ability to extract and be guided by contextual information including social cues.	• Although the specific needs of individual pupils should be addressed in the classroom context it is important to transfer these principles to the wider school environment. This may include: • Pictorial timetables (for some pupils a written timetable will suffice) • Labelling of areas by function, cupboards to indicate contents • Visual aids or systems to enable pupils to indicate they need support E.g. a card that signifies they need time out • Visual menus • Directional arrows to support pupils queuing for lunch etc. • Any no entry areas • Clearly marked exits (This is not an exhaustive list but gives some indication of potential areas for development).

The Impact of ASD on Whole School Approaches	
Impact of ASD	**Responding to the needs of pupils with ASD**
• Stress may lead to pupils behaving in a way that is viewed as being inappropriate, disruptive or generally challenging.	• Promotion of positive perceptions and attitudes towards diversity. • CPD for staff including auxiliary and support staff etc included in any awareness training. • Agreed procedures in relation to behaviour need to be understood by all staff. Such procedures do not need to be complex and could be as simple as staff asking the lead adult if they require assistance. Team approaches to supporting pupils who are displaying challenging behaviour are essential and key/lead staff need to be identified and know they have the support of senior and other colleagues. • Effective support and de-briefing needs to be in place for staff who become involved in difficult or challenging incidents involving pupils. • Approaches to supporting pupil behaviour should take account of the dignity and confidentiality of the pupil. It is important to recognise that inappropriate attention on a pupil may in fact exacerbate the situation. In the longer term this may result in an unjustified reputation that may follow the pupil throughout their school career and beyond. • Opportunities for parents to engage with the wider parent population will be important in developing an inclusive ethos.

The Impact of ASD on Whole School Approaches	
Impact of ASD	**Responding to the needs of pupils with ASD**
• Parents of pupils with ASD will be coping with a range of emotional and practical issues that other parents are unlikely to encounter. Pupils across the spectrum and of all ages are unlikely to share information, concerns or news about their school life. Whilst many people will feel this is typical of all children it is important to recognise that for pupils with ASD this is more likely to be as a result of communication, cognition and social interaction issues that are directly related to ASD.	• Policy and practice that supports effective home/ school communication need to be considered. This should include whole school information as well as specific issues or information that arise in relation to the individual pupil. Respectme, the national anti-bullying service provides support in developing, refreshing and implementing effective anti-bullying policies, practice and training in the prevention of and dealing with bullying.
• Pupils with ASD are vulnerable to bullying. Due to the extreme social naivety of pupils with ASD they are also vulnerable to inadvertently being drawn into bullying behaviour. Pedantic and rigid thinking may also lead to behaviour that others perceive as bullying. Whilst it is difficult to make an accurate assessment anecdotal evidence would suggest that experiencing bullying is by far the predominant issue for pupils on the spectrum.	• Robust anti-bullying policies supported by school ethos and values and effective response to incidents need to be in place and known to all pupils and parents. • Recognition that bullying of children on the spectrum may take many forms is important. Where children with ASD are seen to be bullying or at risk of developing bullying type behaviour it needs to be made clear to them that it is unacceptable, what the consequences of such behaviours are and what the alternatives to this behaviour could be. These messages need to be clear, unambiguous and delivered in a supportive, non - judgemental manner. Good home school liaison will be needed to ensure a consistent message and so that the pupil knows there is communication between both settings. Modern technology can be used to develop approaches that are not time or staff intensive e.g. a home – school e-mail link.

The Impact of ASD on Whole School Approaches	
Impact of ASD	**Responding to the needs of pupils with ASD**
• Pupils with ASD may find it stressful to participate in whole school or larger events such as assembly, outings or sports day. Difficulties can arise from core challenges in autism and also from sensory processing difficulties, anxiety and motivation.	• It will be important for schools to start with the basic premise that all events should be made accessible to pupils and that where possible pupils will be supported to participate. • This needs to be tempered with an understanding of individual needs and skills and that for some pupils an incremental approach will be needed. e.g. attending assembly for 5 minutes then gradually building tolerance.
• For some pupils with ASD academic achievement will be relatively easily attained. Social success and participating as active citizens within the school with a genuine feeling of belonging will be much harder won.	• It is also important to recognise that for some pupils attendance and participation in a range of events may not be realised and indeed it may be counter productive to "force" participation as this may adversely impact on the rest of the day. In some cases it may result in deterioration in confidence or other key areas. Developing practice in this area will require staff to view the event from the perspective of the pupil with ASD. Professional judgement based on detailed knowledge of individual pupils and their targets will direct and guide practice in this area. • Schools will need to take steps in a way that recognising wider achievement. This should not be tokenistic but should be age appropriate and should be part of the promotion of positive behaviour for all pupils. e.g. see example 7, p. 68. • Schools should be aiming for an ethos that recognizes achievement and effort in academic and non academic aspects of school life.

The Autism Toolbox

Part 2
Section 3

Support for Parents and Families

Section 3

Support for Parents and Families

Introduction

This section begins by considering the importance of parents and practitioners working in partnership with each other in the best interests of children and young people. For partnership working to be at its most effective sharing and collaboration are essential: between parents, between professionals and between parents and professionals.

This section links with the following HGIOS Quality Indicators (HGIOS Partnership with Parents Self-evaluation series, HMIE, 2006b) (Resource 30, Resources Section, CD Rom):

2.2 The schools success in involving parents, carers and families

5.7 Partnership with learners and parents

5.8 Care, welfare and development

... and with the HMIE ASD Review Recommendations 6 and 8.

3.1 Working with Parents

Over the last decade government policy has supported and promoted the concept of partnership working (PHIS Report, 2001; '*Getting it right for every child*', 2006c). This partnership is between agencies and professionals as well as families and individuals and is welcome and positive progress. Parents have a number of new rights including having their views considered and to be informed and involved in decision making in a number of aspects of their child's education (Education (Additional Support for Learning) (Scotland) Act 2004; Scottish Schools (Parental Involvement) Act 2006).

This concept however can present particular challenges for parents. How can parents be involved in dialogue, negotiation and decision-making on behalf of their child without relevant information that includes at least a basic knowledge of ASD and of the processes that involve their child?

Parents are correctly recognised as essential in many aspects of their children's education but where the child has an ASD parental participation is crucial. This participation will enable the child to gain the best possible outcomes.

Careful consideration should be given on how the school can best support parents who are awaiting their child's assessment or going through the diagnostic process. The same applies to those parents who choose not to seek a diagnosis for their child.

Parents, like their children, are not a homogenous group and will be at differing stages of acceptance of their child's diagnosis, have varying levels of knowledge and understanding of ASD, and may have widely differing views on approaches and treatments.

What parents can offer the school is unique, detailed, in-depth knowledge of their child over time. Information should be sought from parents as soon as possible and, when added to the formal assessments undertaken by the various professionals, gives a useful and more holistic view of the child. This process should continue throughout their school years and will lead to more effective teaching.

A possible framework for asking parents about their child could include the following questions:

- Are there any activities that your child likes?
- Are there any activities that your child dislikes?
- What is your child good at?
- How does your child prefer to communicate with you?
- Does your child have a particular friend or preferred playmate?
- Does your child have a 'special interest'?
- Are there any particular sensory issues?
- What do you do when your child becomes stressed or distressed?
- Is there anything else that you feel is important for us to know?

Such meetings offer the opportunity for the development of parent/teacher relationships. Parents will feel reassured that the teacher is interested in their child, pleased to be given the opportunity to discuss these issues and to feel their opinions are valued. Listening is a major component in any communication process and 'not being listened to' is a frequent criticism of professionals by parents (Dale, 1996).

For all parents, having a child with ASD was not planned. Parents may have experienced a long and tortuous route to final diagnosis and when they are told that their child has a life-long disability emotions and reactions are complex. What does this mean for their family, and family life, both in the short and long term?

- Coming to terms with the diagnosis is often likened to the grief cycle associated with bereavement - Denial, Anger, Bargaining, Depression, and Acceptance (Kubler-Ross, 1973). Parents will require tolerance and understanding from all those dealing with them and this is especially true during the period following diagnosis.
- For some parents adjusting to the diagnosis is prolonged and difficult and they will

continually return to one particular aspect of the grief cycle. It is also worth noting that whilst some parents can accept the child's disability it would be incorrect to assume they have come to terms with it, no matter how long ago the child received the diagnosis.

- Overwhelming guilt is a common reaction and this may have implications as parents can become overly sensitive to any criticism (actual or perceived) and view it as a comment on their parenting skills. Parents need to be reassured that it is not their fault the child has an ASD.
- As well as coming to terms with, and learning about, their child's difficulties parents also have to grapple with aspects of the education system that are completely new to them.
- It becomes easy to be confused and overwhelmed by the processes and systems, the technical language, the various approaches, roles of different professionals and the complexities of inter-professional working.
- The vast majority of parents care deeply and desperately about their child. They will take time to understand the complex nature of their child's difficulties, particularly in the early days following diagnosis.
- Parents need to feel the school is the best setting for their child to achieve and may spend considerable time and energy exploring various options. Documented evidence of good practice in ASD within the school will be reassuring for parents.
- When working together parents have a right to expect empathy, understanding, mutual respect and tolerance from professionals who in turn have a right to expect mutual respect, civility and recognition of their knowledge and expertise (for more information about parents and professionals working together see Section 6 - Resources 70 and 71).

3.2 Schools' Guidance to Parents - a Reciprocal Relationship?

The average age of a child receiving a diagnosis of autism is approximately five years although those children who are more academically able often have more subtle presentations and may avoid diagnosis until adolescence (Howlin and Moore, 1997).

During the critical period around diagnosis school remains a constant in the child's life, providing regular structure and stability whilst parents and families begin to understand the lifelong implications of such a diagnosis.

Educational professionals may have been involved with the child and parents during the assessment period, or perhaps been part of the diagnostic process and therefore already have an understanding of the parents and extended family. This relationship can be pivotal in helping parents understand how ASD affects their child and impacts on their learning as well as developing strategies that will help.

Parents place clear importance and value on the availability of good quality, relevant up-to-date information. Research evidence on provision of information for parents highlights a number of significant considerations including the timing, content and presentation of any information. Parents also highly value a 'key person' to help them understand the information provided (Mitchell and Sloper, 2000; Mansell and Morris, 2004).

Parents may well look to the school for such a person initially. How is the school going to react to such a demand that will have implications on teacher time? Does the teacher have sufficient knowledge and understanding of ASD to assist these parents? Will the parent/professional relationship be undermined if their child's teacher does not have a basic understanding of ASD? Does the school know where to direct parents for eclectic unbiased information?

Strong multi-disciplinary links with colleagues in health, social services and the third sector can be of significant help in this situation. Is there an ASD Coordinator or a Local Area Coordinator (*Changing Childhood report,* Scottish Executive, 2004b) who could be of assistance?

ASD is a lifelong condition and therefore the information needs of parents and individuals will change over time. There are however specific periods of transition where information provision is particularly helpful:

- At diagnosis
- Starting and changing schools
- At puberty
- Transitions from child to adult services

When an adolescent is diagnosed the challenges for the parents and the school can be particularly complex and have a sense of urgency as the school years are coming to an end. Who explains the autism spectrum to the young person? Where does the young person go for information? Often parents find themselves in the situation of trying to explain these concepts to their child – and should this be the case? Some parents may do this well but others will be too protective to take this action. Parents may look to the school for help in guiding the young person through an understanding of their condition. This is especially true of young people who have a teacher they view as a 'mentor' and particularly trust.

Parents of children who have been diagnosed for a while often become experts in ASD in relation to their child. Many parents will be well read, attend ASD conferences or presentations and some will undertake accredited further education courses in ASD giving them a broader understanding of the condition. How do the teachers feel when dealing with these parents? How can the school best utilise these knowledgeable parents? Could these parents be involved in the provision of in-service education? Perhaps they have acquired resources such as books or DVDs that could be shared?

Recommendation 6 of the HMIE report on Education for Pupils with Autistic Spectrum Disorders provides clear and detailed guidelines on information provision to parents that will help to answer some of the questions posed. Teachers can feel vulnerable when asked questions concerning particular approaches and interventions. Honesty is the best policy. Parents' expectations of professionals' knowledge are usually reasonable and realistic and learning together engenders the 'team approach' to their child.

Parents will seek reassurance and evidence that their child's school is, at the very least, ASD aware. They may also seek information on the skill level of their child's teacher in relation to ASD. Many schools seem reticent in promoting the high level of skills and qualifications in ASD of many of their teaching staff. Perhaps this could be included in the information provided to parents:

- School provides a sense of structure and stability for the child and family, particularly throughout the diagnostic period.
- Teachers may be a first 'port of call' for parents seeking information on ASD.
- High quality, up-to-date information and guidance is crucial in empowering parents.

(See Section 6 - *Resources 57, 58, 63, 66, 70, 71, 74)*

3.3 Communicating Effectively with Parents

Effective, productive partnership working with parents requires some consideration but will always require an effective communication strategy. How do parents react to the notion of partnership? Why do parents react or behave in certain ways? Certainly there will be times when their behaviour may be at odds with their internal feelings, for example:

- An articulate, confident and knowledgeable parent who expects to be treated as an equal may have difficulty admitting a lack of understanding or being unsure of certain specialist aspects of their child's assessments.
- A passive, unquestioning parent who seems to trust all professional judgement may lack confidence in their own abilities but will have un-stated personal opinions about their child's education.
- An angry parent may be well-informed regarding statutory legislation, have high expectations of its implementation and can be confrontational if these expectations are perceived as not being met. This can lead to emotionally charged, tense meetings.

The vast majority of parents really care about their child's welfare and education and their sole aim is to ensure that appropriate and effective provision is in place. They will need evidence and reassurance that the school is meeting their child's needs (Jones, 2002).

Schools need to ensure there is a wide range of communication options open to parents and many schools operate an 'open door policy' displaying a true willingness to engage in and maintain open communication (Stakes and Hornby, 2000).

Children with ASD do not have the easy chatter of normally developing children and rarely discuss their school day. Parents can feel isolated and removed from their child's daily school activities resulting in speculation or inaccurate assumptions on what is actually happening in school. This can result in increased parental stress and anxiety as well as discontent with the school.

Example 18 – Darren

Darren (aged 10) is a young boy diagnosed unequivocally with Asperger's Syndrome. Darren has collected a number of diagnoses since the age of five years including dyspraxia, specific language impairment, and anxiety. This long and complicated route to diagnosis has led to increased parental anxiety and tensions within the wider family. Darren is an only child and lives at home with both parents. He attends his local primary school as do his two younger cousins, Lee-Anne and Stacey. Darren's mum has a prickly relationship with their mum (Joanne) as over the years she has been quite critical of Darren's behaviour. Joanne frequently lets Darren's mum know 'what happened in school' from information gleaned from her young daughters. The story almost always presents Darren in a negative or vulnerable light and distresses mum considerably although she does try to hide her true feelings.

In addition to the whole school communication strategy including websites, handbooks, school and class newsletters, parent teacher meetings, parent prompts etc, parents of children with ASD will require a clear specific communication plan. Communication is a two way process and the school should be made aware of significant home events that may impact on the child. The frequency and methods of ongoing communication should be negotiated with parents, as some will require a higher level of contact or involvement than others.

Regular planned face-to-face meeting to discuss strategies and progress. This should be with the teacher and/or assistant who work with and know the child best.

Home/school diaries. However, be circumspect in what you write as you have no control over who reads the comments or their immediate reaction. The diary should not be a list of negative behaviours. The only effect of this is to increase the anxiety levels of the child and make the parents feel inadequate, dispirited and perhaps angry with the child or the school approach.

Regular telephone contact to share information and good news is quick and useful. Depending on previous experiences some parents may associate a telephone call with 'bad news' e.g. being called to the school because of disruptive behaviour.

Technological advances have the potential to significantly and positively impact on communicating with parents and help to include them in their child's education. Make the technology work for you using E-mail, digital photographs, video diaries, and web logs. Password protected parental access on the school website could show parents their child working and coping in group situations Even telephone technology has the potential to capture particular happy or worthy examples of achievement to share with the parents (Plimley and Bowen, 2006).

Example 19 - Good practice in communicating with parents

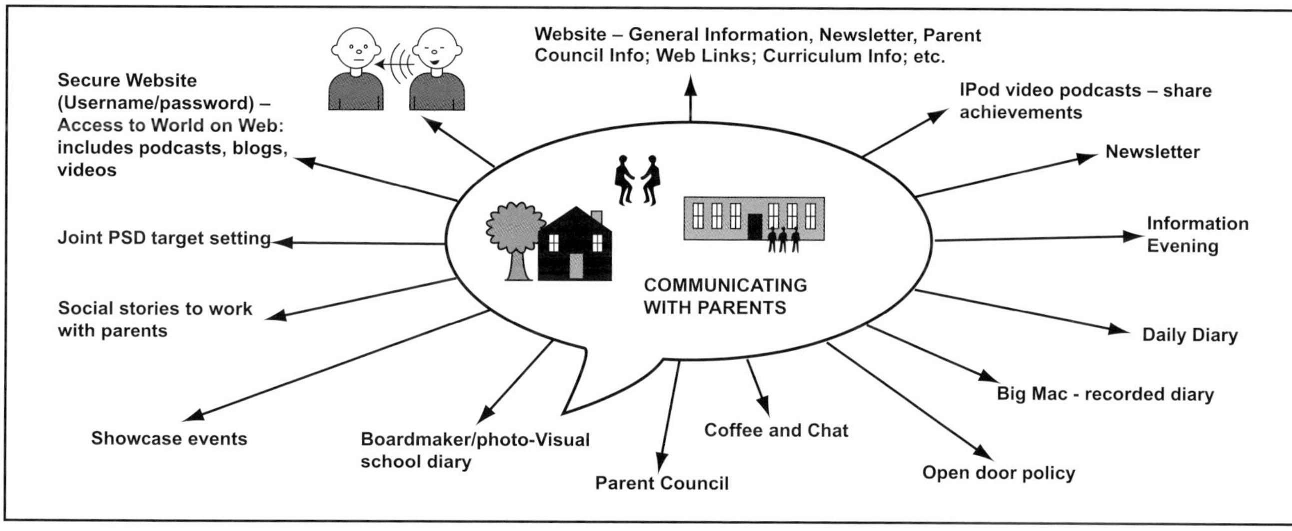

© Isobel Mair School (With thanks)

Evidence of good practice in parent/teacher communication includes that:

- Effective communication is a two way process;
- Communication is enhanced by using successful technology; and
- Effective communication will improve outcomes for the child and family.

Family Diversity

Hatton and Emerson (1999), Emerson, Hatton, Felce, and Murphy (2001) predicted that by 2021, one in ten people with learning difficulties would belong to a non-white ethnic minority group.

Identification rates of the child's disability before school age are much lower in communities originating from the Indian subcontinent living in the UK. It has been proposed that professionals may also contribute to this lowered identification rate. They may recognise the difficulty and simply attribute it to poor language skills, differences in parenting styles or some other factor rather than diagnose it as a disability (Reading, 1999).

Some families from ethnic minorities feel that their beliefs and needs will either be ignored or misunderstood and ridiculed by the white service provider (Shah, 1995).

There is limited research on the understanding of ASD in various ethnic communities (Perepa, 2007). Research highlighted that many languages do not have a word to describe the condition of autism. What is considered as indicative of ASD in the UK, for example looking directly into the eyes of an adult, might be considered as culturally inappropriate in their country of origin where differing social conventions pertain.

Hatton (1999) stated that the level of service uptake among South Asian families is influenced by their ability to speak English and their length of stay in the UK. Shah (1995) identified that that some minority ethnic communities may not be using services because they fear the accusation of taking more than their share.

In attempting to make services accessible it is helpful to identify goals for engagement with all families to understand the issues they face and the barriers that hinder them from accessing services. By developing links to community-based organisations, community and religious groups it may be possible to take information into the community and to advertise services. Audio and visual information to aid understanding of ASD and the ASD services that are available can be held in local libraries. Be aware of the possibility of limited literacy skills and the need to offer alternatives, for example through a telephone interpretation service.

3.4 Meetings with Parents

The rights of parents under the Education (Additional Support for Learning) (Scotland) Act 2004 include:

- Having their views considered and be involved in decision making.
- Having a supporter or advocate present at any discussion or meeting with an education authority when their child's additional support needs are being discussed.

It is importance that professionals are aware of such parental rights, and facilitate their enactment.

Parents of children with an ASD will be involved in numerous formal and informal meetings and reviews throughout their child's education and beyond. A key component of successful partnership between parents and professionals is the quality of these meetings.

Short informal meetings between parents and the class teacher are helpful in problem solving, developing classroom strategies and celebrating success. However, even the most articulate, well-prepared and knowledgeable parents can find large multi professional review meetings difficult, extremely stressful and mentally exhausting. This can be for numerous reasons including:

- Lack of self-confidence
- Lack of information

- Lack of knowledge of the procedures and processes
- Apprehension about their child's progress or behaviour
- Apprehension about professionals judging their parenting skills
- Traumatic experience at previous meetings

Detailed information on good practice in communicating with parents can be found in Chapter 6, Supporting Children's Learning (Scottish Executive, 2005c). However many of these anxieties can be lessened considerably by a few sensible and practical strategies:

- Parents should be advised of their right to have a supporter or advocate present at meetings. This person can be of significant assistance in helping parents to list and then prioritise the topics they wish to be discussed.
- At the pre meeting stage parents should be provided with written information stating the purpose of the meeting, the agenda and time allocated as well as who has been invited.
- To increase the effectiveness of parental input in the review process a form or set of questions could be devised asking for information in specific areas e.g. general health, abilities, self-help skills, behaviour, areas of achievement, areas of concern and home circumstances (Dale 1996). This could assist parents to organise their thoughts on the child's needs and progress and make them feel part of the 'team'.
- Careful consideration should be given to how many people are invited to attend the meeting –are they all necessary? Parents can be overwhelmed and inhibited when confronted by a large group of professionals, particularly if they are not aware of particular professionals roles in relation to their child.
- Any information or papers being considered must be sent out before the meeting. It is unfair and anxiety provoking to expect parents to read and absorb information and then form questions on technical reports presented during meetings.
- All information should be clear and specific with explanation given on any 'jargon' or technical terms. If parents receive clear explanation in layman's terms they will ultimately be empowered to use such terminology (Carr, 2006).
- During the meeting ensure that one person is encouraging active participation from the parents, inviting their views, particularly where options are presented for consideration. The meeting should not hold any nasty surprises for parents with regard to their child's progress or behaviour as these issues should have been dealt with during ongoing informal contact or meetings.
- Parents all too frequently receive only news regarding their child's inappropriate or challenging behaviour so it is vital to celebrate and minute their achievements. The chair should summarise the meeting noting action points and proposed time scales as well as

the person responsible for any implementation. Minutes should be presented to parents as soon as possible.

Building strong relationships between parents and professionals will make it easier to solve disagreements informally (Enquire, 2007) (See Section 6 - *Resource 74*). This approach is far preferable to the added stresses for parents and families of the formal dispute resolution routes:

- Involving parents in the review process will significantly improve the quality of information available.
- Encourage parents to consider involving a supporter or advocate at meetings.
- Positive, realistic meetings involving open discussion with clear outcomes will enhance the parent professional relationship.

3.5 Inclusion of Parents of Children and Young People with ASD in the Life of the School

There is considerable agreement that parental involvement in education has a positive influence on children's learning (HGIOS, HMIE, 2007a. Parents as partners in their children's learning, Scottish Executive, 2006b). Parents can feel isolated from their child's educational experience therefore it is important to offer a range of options on how they can feel, and be, involved in the life of the school. Parents will differ in how much they wish to be involved and this is perfectly normal and similar to all parents. It is important to recognise that bringing up a child with an ASD is a challenging process. This can become all consuming as they attend meetings and appointments, learn about the condition or analyse and implement various approaches. This is in conjunction with, and not in place of, everyday family life.

For most families the only 'respite' they have from the child is whilst they are at school, and even then may worry that the school will contact them with a problem requiring their immediate attendance. It is recognised that children with an ASD are, on average, 20 times more likely to be excluded from school than their peers with one in five of this group excluded at least once (Humphrey and Lewis, 2008). The impact of these exclusions on family life can be considerable:

- Is this a single parent family?
- What happens if the parent is employed?
- Do they have a supportive social or family network to help out?

There may be reluctance from parents to fully engage in school life for a wide variety of reasons including their own educational experiences:

- Do they feel they have anything to contribute?

- Do they feel they are going to be judged by other parents or professionals because of their child's idiosyncratic behaviour?
- Are they embarrassed?
- Are they simply overwhelmed by the circumstances they find themselves in?
- Are they mentally and physically exhausted? Do they have any form of regular respite or break from caring?

Any free time parents have will be precious and perhaps is best spent supporting the needs of the wider family as well as each other. Families need to be supported to stay strong in the face of long-term adversity. Special mention can be made regarding grandparents who may be very involved in the child's life and help support the family in general. Some parents and families will have little left in reserve to consider any regular involvement and this should be recognised and respected:

- Have parents been made aware of the different ways they could be involved and included in their child's school? Is the school ethos open and welcoming for the whole family?
- Does the school have a clear regular communication strategy for sharing information and knowledge with all parents?
- Do parents of the child with ASD feel comfortable and accepted rather than being viewed as overprotective, difficult or risk averse?

There are many varied ways of including parents in school life including:

- At a policy level through their professional expertise, parental representations at Parents forum or council, participation at in-service training for teachers or through active membership of national organisations.
- As a resource within the school or classroom. Many parents, commonly mothers, develop excellent skills in empathising and supporting children on the autism spectrum and some are willing to act as classroom volunteers. This kind of involvement will have pros and cons therefore development of a clear, whole school policy should be considered.
- Supporting their child's learning at home. Parents can support the teacher by reinforcing classroom programmes. This is particular important in supporting children on the autism spectrum to generalise aspects of their learning.

It could be suggested that if parents feel understood and included within the school their child's situation within the school will be comparable. The Parents as Partners in Their Children's Learning: Toolkit (Scottish Executive, 2006) (See Section 6 - Resource 71) is a useful practical resource providing detailed information on supporting partnership with parents in all aspects of their children's learning.

A cornerstone of effective, active partnership arrangements includes providing parents with opportunities to express their views and perceptions as well as enabling them to raise issues of importance to them. This can be achieved through a range of sources including direct contact, interviews, surveys and questionnaires. There will be some parents of children with an ASD who, for a variety of reasons, are difficult to engage however it remains important to seek their views.

When parents are effectively included, teachers gain a more holistic view of the child's home life and parents gain a deeper understanding of how they can support their child's learning:

- Parents may have limited physical or mental reserves to commit unreservedly
- Effective partnership seeks and recognises parents views
- Parental involvement can be on a number of different levels

3.6 Working with Groups of Parents

Partnership working between parents can be of significant value in developing a collaborative ethos between the school and parents and also encourage the development of shared aims. Parent and family involvement can be empowering as they learn new skills, become knowledgeable about the school and learn to communicate more effectively. There are a number of ways this can be encouraged including:

- Regular discussion groups on topics of interest
- Supporting a self help group
- Education and skills interventions
- Involvement in out-of-school social activities
- Parental programmes linked to summer play schemes
- Online forums

A well-recognised method of parents working together would be a self-help group and this could evolve naturally from a regular discussion group.

Support groups provide information and emotional support and help parents cope with the stresses of parenting a child with an ASD. Parents can gain knowledge, learn strategies and develop friendships and social networks, all of which can help strengthen the family. Some members develop advocacy skills and offer to support parents at school meetings.

How can a school assist a parent support group?

- Provide a meeting room

- Help with the 'administration'
- Provide access to a computer/printer
- Promote the group via school website or newsletter
- Offer to teach parents about specific approaches or interventions used in the school

Becoming a member of a support group requires a level of acceptance and acknowledgement of their child's problems and that is an important psychological step down the road that parents must travel. Support groups can be pivotal in helping to organise or encourage parents to access events that increase their knowledge and understanding of ASD.

Parent education is generally associated with improved family outcomes. Parent education and skills training increases the number of intervention hours a child receives and has been shown to help children generalise and maintain what they have learned (Symon, 2001).

The recent SIGN guideline states that education and skills interventions should be offered to parents of all children and young people diagnosed with an ASD (SIGN 98, 2007). In many pre-school settings parent education and intervention skills training is well established with multi-professional staff developing their own ASD specific training scheme for parents to suit local circumstances and resources. Primary and secondary schools have less well developed schemes however parents will benefit from attending ASD specific in-service events that are of relevance to the age and stage of their child. There are a number of ASD specific group training programmes developed and in common use across Scotland (see section 5.4).

A secure school website could allow a parent forum or group discussion board or perhaps access to distance learning materials. This could be especially helpful in remote or rural areas or for parents who have particular difficulty in travelling or finding childminders or carers for a child with an ASD:

- Schools can encourage and support parent groups in a variety of practical ways.
- Parents benefit from continued education and skills training in ASD. There are recognised training courses in ASD for parents involving input from multi professional staff.

Example 20 - Working with groups of parents

A Applying for funding

A group of parents applied for funding to run an ASD specific group-training programme for ten parents of adolescents with ASD. The training was one day each week for six weeks and the school supported the initiative by providing a meeting room and access to catering facilities.

B A workshop on sensory issues

A local ASD support group organised a workshop on how to deal with sensory issues in ASD. Workshop speakers included an occupational therapist and a local teacher. The occupational therapist discussed some of the theory surrounding sensory sensitivities and gave suggestions on equipment and approaches that may help. A local teacher discussed how some of these approaches transferred into a classroom situation. The workshop was held on an in-service day and made available to parents and professionals. This lead to shared learning and a common understanding of the needs of the individual and the challenges for the family and the school.

C Out of school activities

A primary school organised a weekly activity evening for individuals with an ASD and their siblings. A range of supervised activities including drama, dance and crafts were available. Whilst the children were engaged in the activities the parents had the opportunity to have a coffee and chat with each other. This led to the development of a regular summer play-scheme based in the school. Many of the families were involved in the play-scheme as helpers. The play-scheme has encouraged the children and families to access their own community with more confidence. It has also enabled friendships between parents and built stronger social networks for the families.

D Joint training for parents and professionals

A multi disciplinary group of professionals including teachers, psychologists, speech and language therapists, health visitor and two staff members from the local ASD voluntary organisation received training in the National Autistic Society EarlyBird programme. This team could then offer the EarlyBird programme to groups of parents in a flexible and responsive way with minimal waiting time. Early intervention was maximised and parents and families benefited from gaining knowledge and learning practical strategies as well as meeting other parents in a similar situation.

3.7 What Parents May Be Doing at Home

When their child receives a diagnosis on the autism spectrum parents will react in a variety of ways. Information provided by professionals may be sufficient for some parents, however many become information seekers and are faced with a bewildering array of opinions, interventions and approaches from various sources including the media or the internet. Media reporting can be sensationalist, overly negative, often inaccurate and distressing to read. The volume of information available on the internet is simply overwhelming and clearly quantity is no reflection on quality or content. Parents, particularly in the early stages following diagnosis, are extremely vulnerable to those who promote costly 'cures' and miracle programmes. Parents care deeply for their child and are trying to improve the child's ability to learn and function in the world. They are doing what most parents would do-searching for help in a period of need. It is their coping strategy and should be supported and applauded. The majority of parents will not have the academic background or analytical skills to assess the myriad of information on approaches to make a fully informed choice on interventions.

It could be suggested that parents who have no clear source of good quality information and access information in a haphazard way are at risk of following a particular path that has no good evidence base. This has the potential to bring them into conflict with the very professionals and services their child requires for support (education, health and social services). Perhaps the intervention that has the highest profile, or the slickest advertising will attract parents' attention and they may become very focused on its implementation and ask if this could be followed at school as well. Schools and teachers are ideally placed to assist parents in sourcing good quality, eclectic and unbiased information and perhaps to help them interpret such information with regard to their child's particular profile.

Following diagnosis parents feel a sense of urgency and a strong desire to 'do something' to help their child and lessen the impact of their difficulties. As they learn about ASD and some of the interventions a sense of frustration can develop if they think 'the services' are not doing all they can to improve the child's outcomes. This can be a perceived or actual lack of provision.

Many parents find speaking to other parents in a similar situation helpful for sharing ideas, information and mutual support (Jordan and Jones, 1999). It would be useful for your school to have leaflets or contact details of any local groups or individual parents willing to assist other parents.

No one approach is recognised as better than another however the basic principals may be very similar and aim to promote the child's development by either helping them to learn skills or changing the environment to support their learning. Parents should be involved in discussion on how the school deals with these basic principals in relation to their child's learning. This also helps to share good practice and strategies between school and home encouraging positive partnership.

Working together with shared aims is less confusing for the child and will undoubtedly improve the overall outcomes:

- Listen carefully to any requests from parents (even if your initial reaction is negative)
- Respect parents reasons and choices as long as they are not detrimental to the child
- Discuss with the parents the implications for the pupil and the school including whether the approach 'fits' with the whole school policy

Useful websites to recommend to parents

Authoritative websites that will provide quality information and links to helpful sites and resources as well as local groups and services:

The National Autistic Society: www.autism.org.uk

The Scottish Society for Autism: www.autism-in-scotland.org.uk

The Scottish Autism Services Network: www.scottishautismnetwork.org.uk

Contact a Family: www.cafamily.org.uk

Research Autism: www.researchautism.net

(Provides evidenced based information on interventions in autism spectrum disorders. Also provides a section on how to assess information for scientific validity).

Parentzone: www.paretnzonescotland.gov.uk

(For additional websites, see Section 8).

3.8 Issues for Siblings

Living and coping with a child on the autism spectrum can result in increased vulnerability of the whole family including parents, grandparents and siblings. Research shows that families with a child with autism can be socially isolated and often experience high stress levels as a consequence of their care giving responsibilities, the child's cognitive impairment and the need for long term support (SIGN 98, 2007) (See Section 6 – Resource 3).

Some parents and families show great resilience in the face of adversity and crisis and develop coping strategies to deal with the many and varied stressful experiences they encounter. Others will require significant levels of support to help develop these strategies.

Key components in keeping families strong are recognised to include:

- Open, supportive communication between core family members
- Supportive social networks
- Development of practical skills and a positive outlook
- Positive relationships with professionals
- Needs for help being met appropriately by services

There has been increased focus on the impact that a brother or sister with an ASD can have on their siblings as well as the important part that siblings play in the life of the individual with ASD.

There are special demands on children growing up in a household with a child with autism however it should be recognised that, as in all families, the quality of sibling relationships varies widely. The way that the parents and the school work together will have an impact on the siblings, particularly if the children attend the same school.

When the siblings are younger providing them with age appropriate information will help them to understand why their brother or sister is different. A number of booklets have been produced to assist families and professionals with this task (*See Section 6 – Resources 59, 67, 69*).

Teaching siblings some simple skills in how to be a playmate such as praising good play or initiating new games for their brother or sister with autism may help strengthen the bond between them (Harris, 1994).

Parents and teachers may assume a sibling has a reasonable degree of knowledge about ASD but in fact their understanding may be quite limited. Children may have a range of misconceptions and ideas that require clarification and correction (Example 21 - Siblings Jane/Adam).

For many children and young people their overriding worry may be embarrassment caused by the presence of their idiosyncratic sibling who says or does odd things, who may be known as the 'geek' or the 'daftie' and is decidedly un-cool. How do they explain this to their peer group? Is it going to affect their friendships? Are pupils and teachers going to think that they are the same as their sibling? What if their brother ends up in some of their classes? What if he wants to go to the same school dance?

Young people should not feel responsible for their sibling, they should be allowed to develop their own circle of friends and supported in their extra curricular activities. Their achievements should be celebrated.

They may feel overshadowed by their sibling. They are likely to have confusing and conflicting emotions where, at times, they feel intensely protective and responsible for anything that happens at school but feel angry and hostile when their brother does something that irritates them. They may find themselves idolised by their sibling (Attfield and Morgan, 2007). Young people may have feelings of frustration, sadness and resentment at the impact the ASD has on the relationship with their sibling.

The young person may feel unable to discuss any worries with their parents as they witness first hand the problems their parents may have and do not wish to upset them further. Do they have anyone else to talk too? At times, the pressure on the typically developing sibling may be intense. Parental expectation may be overwhelming as they wish this child to achieve and succeed academically where perhaps the child with ASD has not. This could be a focus of rebellion. There will be times where home life can be tense and mentally and physically exhausting, particularly if the child with autism has an irregular sleep pattern or is going through an unsettled phase. This will have an impact on the academic performance of any siblings.

What may help?

- An awareness of their individual situation
- Age appropriate information for all siblings (*See* Section 6 – Resources 59, 67, 69)
- A 'mentor' who can give quality time to the sibling (Guidance teacher, Befriender)
- Siblings workshops

This could be carried out in partnership with appropriate services such as health, social services or the voluntary sector.

Example 21 - Siblings Jane/Adam

Jane is the five-year old sister of Adam, an eight-year old boy with autism.

Adam has been assessed as having a developmental age of three and has recently started to speak although this is mainly echolalia. Adam and Jane attend the same local school.

Adam communicates using visual supports but there are times, particularly when he is tired or anxious, that he can be destructive or throws things. Jane finds this quite frightening and she has been given clear instruction on what to do if this happens at home which is to go and find Mum or Dad.

Whilst in the school play ground Adam had a prolonged and noisy tantrum witnessed by Jane and some of her classmates. Jane overheard one of the other pupils say that Adam had some sort of sickness.

Jane became quite distressed and upset and Mum had to be called into the school. On questioning Jane it became apparent that she was unsure what was expected of her when this happened in school. Jane also thought that 'sickness' was something that could be caught and she too could 'get autism'.

Jane required reassurance and explanation from both the teacher and her parents.

Example 22 - Supporting siblings of pupils on the spectrum

The ASD team in one area are creating lendable and write-on resources for siblings of young people with an ASD.

The aims are:

- To provide siblings of youngsters with ASD with appropriate materials to help understand the needs of their siblings
- To give siblings and parents access to lendable resources for siblings of a young person with an ASD
- To improve the understanding of ASD within family relationships

In order to achieve this, planning meetings were held to discuss the content. A range of resources that can be photocopied have been produced. The team are also sourcing appropriate story and text books. In order to promote the use of resources they have been advertised in the ASD team newsletter and parents have been invited to come and review and discuss materials.

This has resulted in parents using the materials with positive feedback being obtained. Parents' views regarding the suitability of books for loan have been taken into account.

The intention is to continue to advertise the availability of such material via newsletters. Additionally it is hoped that siblings will be enabled to make a contribution to family training events. Such events will be used as an opportunity to further promote the availability of the resources.

(See Section 6 - Resources 56, 59, 60, 67, 69).

The Autism Toolbox

Part 2
Section 4

Working with Other Agencies

Section 4

Working with Other Agencies

This section provides a background to the importance of multi-professional/multi-agency working, and considers the roles of the different people involved in supporting children and young people with ASD and their families.

- *"To get any kind of all-round service, people with autism don't need a High Street full of competing shops; they need a department store where each department is aware of what the others offer and points people in the direction of other services which complement their own."*

(Donna Williams, 1996, p. 50)

4.1 What is Multi-agency Working?

In order to meet the often complex educational, social, behavioural, sensori-motor and health needs of children with autism, input is often required from a variety disciplines. This requires co-ordinated multi-disciplinary working. In a Scottish Executive funded review of the evidence surrounding integrated children's services (not ASD specific) Brown and White (2006) consider the nature of integrated working between services and the overlapping of collective terms used. The range of terms include: 'partnership working, joint working, joined-up working, inter-agency working, multi-agency working, multi-professional working, inter-agency communication, intra and inter-organisational collaboration and collaborative working'.

Although the terminology used across the range of integrated services varies, a range of key themes necessary for effective multi-disciplinary working emerged. Brown and White (2006) identified these key themes as:

- Clear aims and objectives for the group of professionals involved
- Clear roles and responsibilities
- Strong leadership
- Effective systems for communication
- Information sharing and joint planning
- Commitment to the work involved from both management and staff on the front line

In order to achieve effective multi-disciplinary working a number of crucial elements were recognised. These included:

- The need for joint training for staff

- Appropriate staff support and resources
- Monitoring and evaluation of integrated working

A survey of teachers highlighted the need for staff training as an essential element for positive outcomes in multi-agency working. Additionally this survey highlighted that those schools with more training in ASD reported more positive evaluations of inclusion for children on the spectrum. This highlights a need for autism training for essential positive outcomes (Barnard, Broach, Potter and Prior, 2002). The evidence in the Executive Summary of *Exploring the Evidence Base for Integrated Children's Services* (Brown and White, 2006) presents instances of the negative impact on individuals of services not working together. While there appears to be a dearth of evidence of the positive impact of services working in an integrated way, multi-professional models of working are viewed favourably as models of practice due to their ability to:

- Reduce the amount of work duplicated
- Increase opportunities for professional development
- Increase understanding of the role of other professionals
- Provide the necessary range of services for service users (Brown and White, 2006)

A review of multi-agency key worker systems for children with disability and health needs found that those families with key workers reported more positive outcomes, such as reduced stress levels and quicker access to services compared with those without a key worker (Liabo, Newman, Stephens and Lowe, 2001).

A multi-disciplinary core group of professionals from Social Services, Education, Health, parent representatives and the voluntary sector set out guidelines for good practice in delivering autism services within the National Autism Plan for Children (NAPC) (NAS, 2003). The plan makes specific recommendations regarding the diagnostic process and intervention in the early years. This focuses around multi-disciplinary working, including:

- A need for all professionals to be able to recognise the 'alerting' signals of ASD
- The gathering of information relating to the child's development across settings
- Joint multi-agency training in ASD awareness
- IEPs to involve ASD management strategies which can be used by parents and staff
- A key worker identified for each family where a diagnosis of ASD is made
- A commitment to multi-agency working made by budget holders

Based on this evidence, effective multi-agency working is multi-faceted and is more than merely having a child access a range of services and those services communicating with each other. In order to be truly effective, multi-agency working requires good management, adequate resourcing and appropriately trained and skilled staff. The basic tenet should be to provide the best service possible to children and their families (English, 1999).

If we return to the department store analogy, the professionals involved should be aware of the needs of the whole child. This should incorporate the child's family circumstances, the work and roles of other professionals involved, and if necessary supporting the family to seek out and access additional services which complement those already provided. Consideration should be given to individual cases where the needs of children and their families do not fit with the individual remits of the multi-disciplinary support network and the family cannot be sign-posted to an appropriate resource. In such situations there may be a need for flexibility in professional roles, or else face the danger of needs going unmet.

Mechanisms of multi-agency working that work for professionals such as joint meetings with high numbers of attendees and personal involvement of the child may not work for children with ASD, even those considered to be high functioning. This is due to the core deficits of the disorder: social communication, social interaction and social imagination. Some examples of how this may present very real challenges to the child with ASD are listed below:

- Social impairment may manifest in such ways that essential meetings with groups of professionals result in high levels of anxiety and fear.
- The social communicative impairment may result in the child being unable to get their needs across and misunderstanding others' communications.
- Having many professionals directly involved, and developing relationships with new professionals, might be highly stressful. Reasons may include difficulties building relationships and misperceptions of the role of the professional.
- The ability to self reflect and report accurately on their life experiences is likely to be affected.

Providing alternative ways to represent the child's experiences and views at such meetings may be more effective for the child than attending in person. These might include channelling multi-professional input into supporting and involving a core team of individuals whom the child knows and trusts; identifying alternative means of communicating such as the child submitting written information or an identified person advocating on their behalf; pre-meeting sessions to prepare the child for the meeting; offering alternatives to attending the meeting; post meeting translation sessions in order to ascertain the child's understanding of what has taken place; providing increased time and frequency in order to develop a relationship).

4.2 Who Takes the Lead?

In a report on the assessed needs of individuals with ASD, the Public Health Institute of Scotland (PHIS) recommended multi-agency and multi-professional working from diagnosis onward throughout the life of the person with ASD. However, in regard to how this should be implemented, they noted that,

> *"The model for multi-agency collaboration and identification of the lead agency may vary according to local circumstances and, indeed, may vary over time."*
>
> (PHIS, 2001, p. 37)

The report also recommends having 'agency and interagency guidelines and communication structures, defined care pathways and service standards' agreed upon by the agencies involved. Local Authorities may have guidelines for multi-disciplinary working, as might individual agencies, however these can be supplemented by agreements between individuals within a group who have been brought together by the needs of an individual.

4.3 Transitions and Multi-agency Working

It is widely recognised that children with ASD have difficulty with change and transitions. PHIS (2001) accommodates this by recommending that multi-disciplinary working needs to be flexible and seamless where possible, particularly at crucial times of change (e.g. from children's services to adult services). Ongoing multi-professional support for each child should be provided, across the lifespan if necessary and particularly in the period immediately after diagnosis or at times of uncertainty and change such as prior to, between and post-school transitions.

4.4 Multi-agency Systems

The Scottish Executive developed and proposed a framework of support systems for the mental health and wellbeing of children, young people and their families, (Towards a Healthier Scotland, Scottish Office, 1999; Scottish Executive, 2003a, 2003b, 2003c, 2003d, 2004c, 2004d, 2005a) to strengthen individual agency and collective responsibility for identifying and addressing children's needs. These support systems are based on the principle that mainstream services should ensure that children, young people and parents get the learning and support they need to do well. The proposals also suggest that agencies should take responsibility and do all they can, with the help of others, to support the child before referring to another service. This fits with the SNAP report (Scottish Needs Assessment Programme, 2000) recommendation that children's mental health and wellbeing should be "mainstreamed". In order for this strategic aim of mainstreaming mental health services to be met multi-agency dialogue is essential to meet individual needs.

Such mechanisms developed to support inter-agency dialogue included Integrated Assessment, Planning and Recording Framework (IAPRF) (Scottish Executive, 2005a). Some children and young people have particular health, learning, or social needs which require assessment and support from a range of different services and agencies. The system is intended to ensure the consistency and quality of assessments by introducing a common structure for assessing needs, sharing appropriate information, planning and co-ordinating services offered by different professionals and agencies, into a coherent view of a child's strengths and needs. There is an expectation that all professionals will be working to the same frame of reference so that the child's experience is maintained at its centre and that account is taken of strengths, achievements, and the personal resources of the child and family.

A further support system that promotes multi-agency working is the formation of Community Health Partnerships (CHPs). CHPs are intended to provide a focus for service integration and promote:

1. "Horizontal" integration with children's service partners, (i.e. education, social services, youth and community, justice and voluntary sector)
2. The "Horizontal" integration with health service partners (i.e. primary care, community health and secondary care)
3. The "Vertical" integration with specialist mental health services (through local, regional and national networks)

The Mental Health (Care and Treatment) (Scotland) Act 2003 propose *'a range of provisions to secure benefits for, and protect the rights of, people with mental disorder.'* "*Mental disorder*" is defined in the Act as including *'any mental illness, personality disorder or learning disability, however manifested'.* This Act then becomes relevant to people with an ASD whether or not they have a co-morbid condition. The Act's primary objective is to ensure that for those people with mental disorder receive effective care and treatment. This relates to all people with mental disorder, including children and young people.

These different support systems are designed to:

- Meet the range of needs required by those with complex needs
- Provide coherent structures to facilitate inter- and intra-agency working
- Recognise the specialist remits that the range of professionals from a variety of services possess
- Provide a seamless coherent pathway of support to the young person and their family across their life span

4.5 Co-ordinated Support Plans (CSPs)

A Co-ordinated Support Plan (CSP) is a statutory educational planning document. A CSP is compiled for those pupils whose enduring additional support needs arise from one or more complex and/or multiple factors which are likely to continue for more than one year and who require significant support to be provided by an education authority and one or more appropriate agency, namely any other local authority, any health board, Careers Scotland, Further Education Colleges and Higher Education Institutions. The CSP focuses on supporting the child to achieve learning outcomes and assisting the co-ordination of services from the appropriate agencies. However, it is expected that there will only ever be a small number of children and young people with additional support needs that require such a high degree of co-ordination of support from education authorities and appropriate agencies.

Education authorities must have arrangements in place to identify from among those pupils for whose school education they are responsible, those who will require a Co-ordinated Support Plan. When considering whether a Co-ordinated Support Plan may be required, or in preparing such a plan, education authorities must seek and take account of relevant advice and information (including assessments) from appropriate agencies and other persons whom they think appropriate. The Co-ordinated Support Plan should remain adequate and should be monitored and reviewed regularly, at least every 12 months.

A parent has the right to request a CSP and this request may be directed through the child's school or directly to the education authority.

A CSP contains information on the educational objectives for the child or young person; the additional support needed and who will provide the support. Further information about the contents of the Co-ordinated Support Plan is listed below.

The contents of Co-ordinated Support Plans

Individual Details
Parental Details
Profile
Factors giving rise to additional support needs
Nominated School
Parental Comment
Child/Young Person's Comment
Co-ordinated Support Plan Review Timetable
Education Authority Contact Points
Parental Advice and Information on the co-ordinated support plan

The CSP template can be viewed on page 123 of the Scottish Government (2005c) Supporting Children's Learning: Code of Practice or by accessing the Scottish Government *Supporting Children's Learning: Code of Practice* electronically-
http://www.scotland.gov.uk/Publications/2005/08/15105817/58319

4.6 Top Ten Points for Positive Practice in Multi-agency Working

1 Make use of the support structures that exist to facilitate inter-agency working. Usually, all authorities contain an 'expert' in the field. Make connections and tap into existing resources.

2 Be aware of existing national and local authority guidelines on multi-agency / multi-professional working.

3 Know what resources are available to those within your local authority. This information will enable you to signpost families to services with the goal of meeting the young person's needs. Links with external agencies may be beneficial for securing appropriate support in a timely way and names as well as contact numbers can help parents to reach the right individuals.

4 Identify, consult and agree who or which agency should or could take responsibility for co-ordinating multi-disciplinary working. Remember the key nature of personal micro and macro transitions by recognising that this agency may change over time according to the needs of the child and local circumstances. A 'key-worker' from any discipline can be identified to take responsibility for management of support, particularly at times of transition. Experience indicates that in multi-disciplinary work it is essential to have someone identified as having a lead overview responsibility. In the *Getting it Right for Every Child* programme such a person is termed the 'lead professional'. In each case, thought will be needed on who can best fulfil that role, and whether that is the practitioner working most directly with the child and family, or someone with a broader overview; much will depend on individual circumstances.

5 Establish clear objectives for the group of professionals around a child and define clear roles and responsibilities for the agencies involved. Skills such as effective chairing and co-ordinating of multi-agency meetings are essential to this process.

6 Be flexible and persistent. If a child with autism or their family has a need which does not fall within the remit of professionals involved, or their needs become increasingly complex, seek additional alternatives. If alternatives cannot be signposted for the family, some flexibility in roles may be required, or else there may be a real risk of needs going unmet.

7 Whilst the provision of services and support should be needs led rather than diagnosis led, professionals involved in multi-agency working should have a good knowledge of ASD and how it impacts on the child's daily life and learning. Responses to an assessed need for the child should also take into account the strengths and needs of the family.

8 Recognise that when involving the child with Autism Spectrum Disorder in planning for service provision, the core deficits of ASD are likely to render typical mechanisms for consultation, such as meetings, self-reflection, and building relationships with external professionals, difficult for the child with ASD. Alternative ways of gaining this information may be necessary if they are to be effective.

9 Recognise that the skills and training of those involved in the multi-disciplinary working are vital to improving outcomes for children and provide appropriate training, e.g. in early identification and specialist supports for those on the autism spectrum. This may be provided by one of the agencies involved, or by an external agency and joint training may be beneficial.

10 Focus on the process of multi-agency working should not detract from the goal of delivering the best possible service to children with ASD and their families. Multi-agency working is a means to achieve this goal.

4.7 Multi-agency Involvement: Professional Roles

If we look at the pupil with an Autism Spectrum Disorder it may be surprising to see the variety and the extent of professionals involved within their support network. Therefore, when supporting a pupil with ASD it may be appropriate to consider the multi-professional context that the person and the family face. Who then, might be involved in the wider support network? What role can professionals as individuals fulfil for the person with ASD and how can they work together? Some of the professionals who may come into contact with the person are listed below:

- **Autism Outreach Teacher** – can provide education consultation and training on an outreach basis to schools supporting pupils with an ASD and they may also observe and assess the pupil prior to this.
- **Arts Therapist** – (Music Therapist, Drama Therapist) can support the child to use art, drama or music as a medium to express or make sense of feelings, to be able to respond and relate to the therapist and others within the safety of the therapeutic relationship or to share and work on any issues that are challenging them, without using words. Governed by their own professional bodies, anyone including parents can refer to an arts therapist (as defined by the Scottish Government under the Allied Health Professionals banner).
- **Autism Networker** – professionals, who have joined the Scottish Autism Service Network with the intention to share good practice, learn from each other and observe key principles of participation.
- **Befrienders** – can provide an additional social support for the person plus they can informally provide short respite to the family. A befriender may be preferable for some children with ASD who have difficulty socialising as the planned interaction is on a 1:1 basis, rather than a group context. This service can be provided by voluntary agencies or Social

Work services, and often the befrienders are volunteer workers.

- **Behaviour support staff** – can provide knowledge of behaviour management techniques to support the child in class and also how these might be adapted for the home.

- **Care Managers –** the role of Care Managers is focused on meeting the needs and of supporting people in their own homes. In practice wider aims of community care or aspects of the care management process may apply. The majority of Care Managers in Scotland are Social Work trained.

- **Children's Panel / Children's Hearing** – when a child commits a crime, the case goes to the Procurator Fiscal. The Procurator Fiscal decides whether to dispose of the case, send the case to court or to a children's Panel. Relevant individuals such as **family members**, **Youth Worker, Social Worker or Teacher**, may be involved, although numbers are kept to a minimum. A hearing into the incident will be heard by a **Panel** of three individuals, trained by the hearing system, and if the child admits the crime, a decision will be made as to how to proceed. This could lead to Social Work involvement, a child protection order, a supervision requirement, other requirements or there may be no further action. The outcome will be dependent on the crime - and in the case of children with autism links with other services and professionals may be important. If the child denies the crime it goes back to court as a children's referral and the Sheriff will decide whether the child is guilty or not after hearing the evidence. A guilty verdict may result in the case getting sent back to the panel, who will make a decision about how to proceed. The children's **Reporter** is responsible for ensuring that the Panel meetings follow the established legal procedures and rules. The child may be appointed a '**Safeguarder**' to act in their interests following a children's hearing. Children's panels may also occur if the child is experiencing difficulties in their life. This can arise if a pupil with ASD has an extended period of time refusing to attend school (information gained from dialogue with legal professional).

- **Child and Adolescent Mental Health** (CAMHs) teams – (including **Clinical Psychologists, Child and Adolescent Psychiatrists, Nurse Therapists, Occupational Therapists, Mental Health Workers**) – can work in partnership with Social Work, Education and Health teams to promote mental health awareness and good practice and provide consultation to these agencies. Can provide assessment and intervention for children and adolescents with mental health problems ranging from behavioural difficulties to severe, complex and persistent mental health disorders. Often Community Mental Health workers provide initial assessment and brief intervention for mental health problems, whilst multi-disciplinary CAMHs professionals will tend to work with more severe and complex cases.

- **Class Teacher** – may be the first point of contact for parents or the child if they are experiencing difficulties with their education or school life.

- **Community Learning Disabilities Nursing Service** – can help with: managing challenging behaviour, continence management, sleep management, promoting independent living skills, health promotion, sexual health education and more, including supporting parents and carers and collaborative working with, or referring to other agencies as appropriate. They can also support the transition to adult health services.
- **Clinical psychologist** – is a mental health professional who aims to reduce psychological distress and enhance and promote psychological well being. They use psychological techniques and methods to enable clients to make positive changes in their lives. Clinical psychologists can work with any particular age group and some specialise in working with children and adolescents, including those who have difficulty with behaviour and or relationships with others.
- **Community Paediatrician –** (evolved from school doctors, links with school nurses) – assessment diagnosis and follow up of children with needs including emotional and behavioural difficulties, physical difficulties, learning difficulties, sensory impairments (deaf/ blind).
- **Community Police –** Community constables provide a vital link between the public and the police. Covering the entire force area, each officer works in the heart of their community carrying out a wide range of activity and work.
- **Counsellor** - may work within a school, in a community based health team or with a voluntary agency. The person should not be sent to counselling, but request counselling. A counsellor sees a client in a private and confidential setting to explore any difficulties the client may be having, distress they may be experiencing or perhaps their dissatisfaction with life, or loss of a sense of direction and purpose (adapted from British Association of Counselling and Psychotherapy).
- **Dietician –** a dietician provides advice, information and teaching on nutrition and diets. Referrals can be made by GPs and hospital consultants. They work with parents, professionals and the general public. More information on the role of the dietician in the health of individuals with ASD can be found on www.autismfile.com/nutrilink.htm.
- **Early Years and Childcare Services** – co-ordinated by Educational Psychology in some instances – meet regarding the needs of pre-school children with Additional Support Needs (ASN) to discuss appropriate placements. These are multi-agency from Health, Education and Social Work (for example Dundee City Council).
- **Education Officer** – may become involved if child is refusing to attend school.
- **Educational psychologist** – assess and advise on matters relating to education such as placement, ways of teaching skills, ways of changing behaviour and providing insight into child's development. For the child with ASD this may also involve training staff in

appropriate support and understanding diagnosis, possibly direct intervention on occasion, as well as advising on approaches that might work in the home.

- **Guidance teacher** – ten standards as outlined by 2004 review of guidance services. In summary, the guidance teacher aims to be an individual that: the child can come to in confidence, can liaise between external agencies and the child/school, can help the child with transition and planning for the future, and can help children understand choices and make informed decisions. A major role of the guidance teacher is to ensure that when a pupil raises a problem, action is taken to help them.

- **Head Teacher** – responsible for whole school policy and approaches. Often a point of contact if concerns have been raised with a class teacher and these have either not been resolved or require further action. The Head Teacher is often the **Link Person** for services such as Educational Psychology.

- **Health Visitors** and **School Nurses** – should be consulted about health issues in the first instance. Links with Social Work, Education, Health and Voluntary sector workers.

- **Local Area Co-ordinator** – the role of the Local Area Co-ordinator varies from authority to authority, with some taking only adults, some only children, some not working for people with Asperger's Syndrome, and some taking these cases on. The function of the LAC is not to be a case manager or to co-ordinate services, but to use knowledge of local groups and services to be able to link children with learning disabilities and their families to the services that they need.

- **Mediation Services** – *'Mediation provides an option for avoiding, resolving or narrowing the area of disagreement between the authority and parents or young people belonging to the area of the authority. It allows disputing parties to seek to resolve their differences with the assistance of a mediator"* (Supporting children's learning: code of practice', Scottish Executive, 2005). A variety of mediation services are available throughout Scotland for a variety of issues, from family mediation to neighbour disputes. Of particular relevance to children with ASD and their families might be the Scottish Mediation Network, which provides a range of helpful publications, and Resolve: ASL, an independent mediation service run by Children in Scotland. Issues discussed can include: exclusion, provision of placement, level of support and provision of transport. The mediator is independent of parents and other parties and their role is to facilitate discussion and assist parties to find a mutually agreeable conclusion. Helpful web links are provided in Section 8.

- **Mental Health Worker – see CAMHs team.**

- **Occupational Therapist** – aims through working with the child, parents and carers, to assess and develop the child's social and practical skills to enable them to function in their daily life. (Not just physical, but social and psychological also. Occupational Therapists can be based in hospitals or community based multi-disciplinary teams (CAMHs or

Learning Disabilities integrated teams) and also within schools, as outlined by the Scottish Government's information on Allied Health Professions – see Section 6 – Resource 10 (Scottish Executive, 2005d).

- **Parents** – the majority of professional services indicate that they require parental permission for referrals and most list working with parents as one of their key functions. The Family Law (Scotland) Act 2006 and the Scottish Schools (Parental Involvement) Act 2006 lay out rights and responsibilities for parents of all children including those with ASN (see also Section 3 – Support for Parents and Families).
- **Parent Liaison Officer** – can be contacted if parents have raised concerns with class teachers and support for learning teachers/or head teachers and feel that these concerns are still an issue.
- **Peers** – either in an informal capacity as social support or to model appropriate behaviour or in a formal capacity as a buddy, reading partner, with a circle of friends or another way that the school uses peers as support.
- **Play Therapist** – can help children understand their feelings and upsetting events that they haven't had the chance to sort out properly. Rather than having to explain what is troubling them, as adult therapy usually expects, children use play to communicate at their own level and at their own pace, without feeling interrogated or threatened.
- **Respite Workers -** generally provide for short break services for carers and the people they care for, with a focus on the right break at the right time and in the right place.
- **School Nurse** – intended as the first point of contact for parents, educators and pupils for all matters related to health. Ways this is done: Questionnaires to all pupils when they start school and prior to the transition to secondary to pick up health problems; educating staff about specific health problems and promoting good health; providing advice to individual pupils upon request; health promotion activities including sexual health and building confidence; vaccinating children; giving advice on issues such as bedwetting and in some cases knowledge of parental support groups.
- **Siblings –** can provide a similar supporting role as listed for peers, or they may take on a more informal 'advocacy' role.
- **Social Workers** – Social Work services may become involved if a child has a need relating to their home or community life that is going unmet. Social Workers, usually from children and families teams, can work either directly with the child to assess their need and arrange appropriate support or can work with parents to increase their ability to care for their child.
- **Speech and language therapist –** paediatric speech and language therapists may be concerned with the development of speech and communication and also eating, drinking and swallowing skills.

- **Support assistants / Auxiliary** - can help with issues like getting around school, focusing on class work.
- **Youth Workers** – provided from a number of sources, including youth centres or clubs. Can organise leisure and play activities, but also work with children who are experiencing problems. Very broad term encompassing those who volunteer, such as Scout leaders, to those who work for Councils and Youth Centres. The general aims of youth workers are to promote well-being and to support the social and personal development of young people and teach responsibility and participation in the community.

Toolbox References

Ainscow, M. (2008) *Centre for Studies on Inclusive Education.* Available at: www.csie.org.uk [Accessed February 2009].

American Psychiatric Association (1994) *Diagnostic and Statistical Manual of Mental Disorders.* 4th Edition. Washington, DC: American Psychiatric Association.

American Psychiatric Association (2000) *Diagnostic and Statistical Manual- IV- Text revision.* Washington, DC: American Psychiatric Association.

Asperger, H. (1991) [1944] Autistic psychopathology in childhood. In: U. Frith (1989) (Ed.) *Autism and Asperger Syndrome.* Cambridge: University Press.

Assessment is for Learning (2006) Learning and Teaching Scotland. Available at: www.ltscotland.org.uk/assess/ [Accessed February 2009].

Attfield, E. and Morgan, H. (2007) *Living with Autistic Spectrum Disorders. Guidance for Parents, Carers and Siblings.* London: Paul Chapman.

Attwood, T. (2007) *The Complete Guide to Asperger's Syndrome.* London: Jessica Kingsley.

Baird, G., Simonoff, E., Pickles, A., Chandler, S., Loucas, T., Meldrum, D. et al. (2006) Prevalence of disorders of the autism spectrum in a population cohort of children in South Thames: the Special Needs and Autism Project (SNAP), *Lancet* 368 (9531), 210–5.

Barnard, J., Broach, S., Potter, D. and Prior, A. (2002) *Autism in Scotland's Schools: Crisis or Challenge?* London: National Autistic Society. Available at: www.nas.org.uk/nas/jsp/polopoly.jsp?d=422anda=4928 [Accessed February 2009].

Barnard, J., Prior A. and Potter, D. (2000) *Inclusion and autism: is it working?* London: National Autistic Society. Available at: www.nas.org.uk/nas/jsp/polopoly.jsp?a=3462andd=160 [Accessed February 2009].

Baron-Cohen, S. (1990) Do autistic children have obsessions and compulsions? *British Journal of Clinical Psychology,* 28, 351-360.

Batten, A. and Daly. J. (2006) *'make school make sense'. Autism and education in Scotland: the reality for families today.* Glasgow: National Autistic Society.

Bee, H. and Boyd, D. (2003) *The Developing Child.* 10th Edition. Boston, MA: Allyn and Bacon.

Bee, H. and Boyd, D. (2008) *Lifespan Development.* 5th Edition. London: Allyn and Bacon, Pearson Education.

Beyer, J. and Gammeltoft, L. (1999) *Autism and Play.* London: Jessica Kingsley.

Bogdashina, O. (2003) *Sensory Perceptual Issues in Autism and Asperger Syndrome.* London: Jessica Kingsley.

Bondy, A. and Frost, L. (1994) The Picture Exchange Communication System. *Focus on Autistic Behaviour,* 9, 1-19.

Booth, T. and Ainscow, M. (2002) *The Index for Inclusion.* The Centre for Inclusive Education. Available at: www.csie.org.uk/ [Accessed February 2009].

Brown, K. and White, K. (2006) *Exploring the Evidence Base for Integrated Children's Services.* Scottish Executive Education Department web publication. Available at: www.scotland.gov.uk/Publications/2006/01/24120649/0 [Accessed February 2009].

Carr, S. (2006) *Technical jargon; an approach, an idea and an offering.* Plain Language Commission. Available at: www.clearest.co.uk [Accessed February 2009].

Centre for Disease Control and Prevention (CDC) (2007) *Prevalence of Autism Spectrum Disorders-Autism and Developmental Disabilities Monitoring Network, Six Sites, United States.* Available at: www.cdc.gov/mmwr/preview/mmwrhtml/ss5601a1.htm [Accessed February 2009].

Charlop-Christy M.H., Carpenter, M., Le L, LeBlanc, L.A. and Kellet, K. (2002) Using the picture exchange communication system (PECS) with children with autism: Assessment of PECS acquisition, speech, social-communicative behaviour, and problem behavior. *Journal of Applied Behavior Analysis*, 35(3): 213-231.

Charter of Rights for People with Autism. (1996) Adopted as a Written Declaration by the European Parliament on May 9th, 1996. Available at: www.autismeurope.org/portal/Default.aspx?tabid=30 [Accessed February 2009].

Christie, P., Newson, E., Newson, J. and Prevezer, W. 1992: An interactive approach to language and communication for nonspeaking children. In Lane, D.A. and Miller, A., editors, *Child and adolescent therapy: a handbook*. Buckingham: Open University Press.

Cumine, V., Leach, G. and Stevenson, G. (1998) *Asperger's Syndrome: A Practical Guide for Teachers*. London: David Fulton.

Cumine, V., Leach, G. and Stevenson, G. (2000) *Autism in the Early Years*. London: David Fulton.

Dahle Bowen, K. and Gargiulo, R. (2004) Asperger Disorder: A primer for early childhood educators, *Early Childhood Special Education Journal*, 32:3,199-203.

Dale, N. (1996) *Working with Families with Special Needs*. East Sussex: Brunner-Routledge.

Dalrymple, N. J. (1995) Environmental Supports to Develop Flexibility and Independence. In: K. A. Quill (Ed.) *Teaching children with autism: Strategies to enhance communication and socialization*. New York: Delmar Publishers Inc.

Dennison, S. (2000) A Win-Win Peer Mentoring and Tutoring Program: A Collaborative Model. *The Journal of Primary Prevention*, 20, 3, 161-174.

Disability Discrimination Act 1995(DDA) (as amended by the Special Educational Needs and Disability Act 2001) (SENDA) Available at: www.opsi.gov.uk/Acts/acts2001/en/ukpgaen_20010010_en_1 [Accessed February 2009].

Disability Discrimination (Public Authorities) (Statutory Duties) (Scotland) Regulations 2005. Available at: www.opsi.gov.uk/legislation/scotland/ssi2005/20050565.htm [Accessed February 2009].

Disability Equality Duty (DED) 2006. Available at: www.dotheduty.org/ [Accessed February 2009].

Division TEACCH (2006) *Treatment and Education of Autistic and related Communication-handicapped Children*. University of North Carolina. Available at: www.teacch.com [Accessed February 2009].

Dunlop, A.W.A., Knott, F. and MacKay, T. (2002) *Developing Social Interaction and Understanding in Individuals with Autistic Spectrum Disorders:* SEED Innovation Grant Funding in Collaboration with The National Autistic Society.

Dunlop, A-W., Knott, F. and MacKay, T. (2007) Developing Social Interaction and Understanding in High Functioning Individuals with Autism Spectrum Disorder. In E. McGregor, M. Núñez, K. Williams, J-C. Gómez, *An Integrated View of Autism: Perspectives from Neurocognitive, Clinical and Intervention Research*. London: Blackwells.

Education (Disability Strategies and Pupils' Educational Records) (Scotland) Act 2002. Available at: www.opsi.gov.uk/legislation/scotland/acts2002/asp_20020012_en_1 [Accessed February 2009].

Edwards, L. (2003) *Promoting Young People's Wellbeing: A Review of Research on Emotional Health.* Glasgow: SCRE, University of Glasgow.

Emerson, E., Hatton, C., Felce, D. and Murphy, G. (2001) *Learning Disabilities: The Fundamental Facts.* London: The Foundation for People With Learning Disabilities.

English, A. (1999) Working together: a multi-agency approach to supporting parents of children with autism, *Good Autism Practice,* April, 3-15.

Enquire (2007) *The parents guide to additional support for learning*. Available at: www.enquire.org.uk/pcp/pub/pcpguides.php [Accessed February 2009].

Fombonne, E. (2005) Epidemiology of autistic disorder and other pervasive developmental disorders, *Journal of Clinical Psychiatry*, 66 (Supp 10): 3-8.

Frith, U. (1989) *Autism: Explaining The Enigma.* Oxford: Basil Blackford.

Ghaziuddin, M., Wieder-Mikhail, W. and Ghaziuddin, N. (1989) Co-morbidity of Asperger Syndrome: a preliminary report, *Journal of Intellectual Disability Research,* 42, 279-283.

Gray, C. (1998) Social Stories and Comic Strip Conversations with students with Asperger Syndrome and High Functioning Autism. In: E. Schopler, G. Mesibov and L. Kunce (Eds.), *Asperger Syndrome or High Functioning Autism?* (pp. 167-198) New York: Plenum Press.

Gray, C. (2002) *My Social Stories Book*. London: Jessica Kingsley.

Greig, A. and MacKay, T. (2005) Asperger's Syndrome and cognitive behaviour therapy: new applications for educational psychologists. *Educational and Child Psychology*, 22, 4, 4-15.

Hanbury, M. (2007) Positive *Behaviour Strategies to Support Children and Young People with Autism.* London: Sage.

Hare, D. (2004) Developing cognitive behavioural work with people with ASD. *Good Autism Practice, 5,* 18-22.

Harris, L. (2000) Your Child's Development. In: M.D. Powers (Ed.) *Children with Autism: a Parents' Guide*. Bethesda: Woodbine House Inc.

Harris, S. (1994) *Siblings of children with Autism: A Guide for Families.* Bethesda: Woodbine House Inc.

Hatton, C. and Emerson, E. (1999) Towards equity in service provision-commentary, *Tizard Learning Disability Review,* 4, 4, 16-19.

Hay, D., Payne, A. and Chadwick, A. (2004) Peer relations in childhood, *Journal of Child Psychology and Psychiatry*, 45, 84-108.

Heimann, M., Nelson, K.E., Tjus, T. and Gillberg, C. (1995) Increasing reading and communication skills in children with autism through an interactive multimedia computer program. *Journal of*

Autism and Developmental Disorders, 25(5):459-80.

Her Majesty's Inspectorate of Education (2006a) *Education for Pupils with Autism Spectrum Disorder*. Livingston: HMIE. Available at: www.hmie.gov.uk/documents/publication/epasd.html [Accessed February 2009].

Her Majesty's Inspectorate of Education (2006b) How Good is Our School. Self Evaluation Series. Partnership with Parents.

http://www.hmie.gov.uk/documents/publication/hgiospwp.pdf [Accessed February 2009].

Her Majesty's Inspector of Education (2007a) *How Good is Our School? The Journey to Excellence Part 3*. Livingston: HMIE. Available at: www.hmie.gov.uk/documents/publication/hgiosjte3.html [Accessed February 2009].

Her Majesty's Inspector of Education (2007b) *The Child at the Centre: Self –evaluation in the Early Years*. Livingston: HMIE. Available at: www.scotland.gov.uk/Publications/2000/06/6177/File-1 [Accessed February 2009].

Hetzroni, O.E. and Tannous, J. (2004) Effects of a computer-based intervention program on the communicative functions of children with autism. *Journal of Autism and Developmental Disorders*, 34(2):95-113.

Hewett, D. and Nind, M. (1998) Introduction: Recent Developments in Interactive Approaches. In D. Hewett and M. Nind (eds) *Interaction in Action: Reflections on the Use of Intensive Interaction*. London: David Fulton Publishers.

Hobson, R, P. (1993) *Autism and the Development of Mind*. Hove, UK: Lawrence Erlbaum.

Hodgdon, L. (1995) *Visual strategies for improving communication.* Michigan: Quirk Roberts Publishing.

Hodges, E., Malone, J. and Perry, D. (1997) Individual risk and social risk as interacting determinants of victimization in the peer group, *Developmental Psychology,* 32, 1033-1039.

Howlin, P., Moore. A. (1997) Diagnosis in autism. A survey of over 1200 patients in the UK, *Autism,* 2, 135-162.

Humphrey, N. (2004) The Death of the Feel-Good Factor? Self-Esteem in the Educational Context, *School Psychology International*, 25, 3, 347-60.

Humphrey, N. and Lewis, S. (2008) 'Make me normal': The views and experiences of pupils on the autistic spectrum in mainstream schools, *Autism. The International Journal of Research and Practice,* 12, 1.

Irlen, H. (1995) Viewing the world through rose tinted glasses. *Communication,* 29, 8-9.

Ives, M. and Munro, N. (2002) *Caring for a Child with Autism: A Practical Guide for Parents*. London: Jessica Kingsley.

Jackson, L. (2002) *Freaks, Geeks and Asperger Syndrome. A User Guide to Adolescence*. London: Jessica Kingsley.

Jones, G. (2002) *Educational Provision for Children with Autism and Asperger Syndrome. Meeting Their Needs*. London: David Fulton.

Jordan, R. (1995) *Computer Assisted Education for Individuals with Autism.* Autism and Computer Application, Autisme France 3rd International Conference.

Jordan, R. (1999) *Autistic Spectrum Disorder: An Introductory Guide for Practitioners.* London: David Fulton.

Jordan, R. (2002) *Autistic Spectrum Disorders in the Early Years: A Guide for Practitioners.* Litchfield: QEd Publications.

Jordan, R. (2004) *Meeting the needs of children with autism in the early years.* New South Wales Autism Society. Sydney.

Jordan, R. and Jones, G. (1999) *Meeting the Needs of Children with Autistic Spectrum Disorders.* London: David Fulton.

Jordan, R. and Powell, S. (Eds.) (1997) *Autism And Learning. A Guide to Good Practice*. London: David Fulton.

Kanner, L. (1943) Autistic Disturbances of Affective Contact, *Nervous Child, 2*: 217-250.

Kaufman, B. N. (1976)*Son Rise*. New York: Warner Books.

Kaufman, B.N. (1994) *Son Rise: The Miracle Continues.* Tiberon, CA: H.J. Kramer Inc.

Kellet, M. (2004) Intensive interaction in the inclusive classroom: using interactive pedagogy to connect with students who are hardest to reach. *Westminster Studies in Education,* 27 (2), 175-188.

Kim, J., Szatmari, P., Bryson, S., Streiner, D.L. and Wilson, F.J. (2000) The prevalence of anxiety and mood problems among children with autism and Asperger syndrome, *Autism,* 4, 2, 117-132.

Klin, A., Volkmar, F., and Sparrow, S. (2000) *Asperger Syndrome.* London: Guilford Press.

Knott, F. and Dunlop, A-W., (2007) (2nd edition) Developing *social interaction and understanding: a resource for working with children and young people with autism.* London: National Autistic Society. Available at: http://www.autism.org.uk/nas/jsp/polopoly.jsp?a=14482&d=542 [Accessed February 2009].

Kubler- Ross, E. (1973) *On Death and Dying.* Oxford: Routledge.

Lamarine, R.J. (2001) Asperger Syndrome. Advice for School Personnel, *Preventing School Failure*, 45, 4, 148-152.

Lawson, W. (2001) *Understanding and Working with the Spectrum of Autism.* London: Jessica Kingsley.

Learning and Teaching Scotland, Scottish Qualifications Authority and Scottish Executive. (2006) *Assessment is for Learning Self Assessment Toolkit.* Glasgow: Learning Teaching Scotland.

Legoff, D. (2004) Use of LEGO© as a therapeutic medium, *Journal of Autism and Developmental Disorders,* 34, 5, 557-571.

Legoff, D. and Sherman, M. (2006) Long-term outcome of social skills intervention based on interactive LEGO© play, *Autism,* 10, 4, 317-329.

Liabo, K., Newman, T., Stephens, J., and Lowe, K. (2001) A Review of Key Worker Systems for Disabled Children and the Development of Information Guides for Parents. Cardiff: Wales Office of R and D for Health and Social Care. In: K. Brown and K. White (2006) *Exploring the Evidence Base for Integrated Children's Services*, Scottish Executive Education Department web publication. Available at: www.scotland.gov.uk/Publications/2006/01/24120649/0 [Accessed February 2009].

Little, L. (2002) Middle Class Mothers' perceptions of peer and sibling victimization among children with Asperger's Syndrome and non-verbal learning disorders, *Issues in Comprehensive Paediatric Nursing,* 25, 1, 43-57.

Lord, C. and Schopler, E. (1994) TEACCH services for preschool children. In S. L. Harris and J. S. Handleman (Eds.), *Preschool education programs for children with autism* (pp. 87-106) Austin, TX: Pro-Ed.

Lovaas, O.I. (1987) Behavioral treatment and normal education and intellectual functioning in young autistic children. *Journal of Consulting and Clinical Psychology,* 55, 3-9.

Lovaas, O.I. (1981) *Teaching Developmentally Disabled Children. The 'me' book.* Baltimore: University Park Press.

MacKay, T.A.W.N. and Dunlop, A.W.A. (2004) *The Development of a National Training Framework for Autistic Spectrum Disorders, A Study of Training for Professionals Working in the Field of ASD in Scotland.* Glasgow: National Autistic Society and University of Strathclyde.

Marwick, H., Dunlop, A-W. and Mackay, T. (2006) *A Literature Review of Autism for Her Majesty's Inspectorate of Education (HMIE) towards Evaluation of The Educational Provision for Children With Autistic Spectrum Disorders in Scotland.* Available at: www.hmie.gov.uk/Publications.aspx [Accessed February 2009].

Mansell, W. and Morris, K. (2004) A survey of parents' reactions to the diagnosis of an autism spectrum disorder by a local service, *Autism,* 8, 4, 387-407.

Mitchell, W. and Sloper, P. (2000) *User- friendly information for families with disabled children: A guide to good practice.* Joseph Rowntree Foundation. Available at: www.jrf.org.uk/knowledge/findings/socialcare/n30.asp [Accessed February 2009].

Mortlock, J. (1993) *Socio-sexual development of people with autism* (based on a presentation given at an Inge Wakehurst Trust study weekend, Nov 1993) Available at: www.nas.org.uk/nas/jsp/polopoly.jsp?d=364anda=2187 [Accessed February 2009].

National Autistic Society (2006) *National Autistic Society Fact Sheet - Mental Health and Asperger syndrome.* Available at:

www.nas.org.uk/nas/jsp/polopoly.jsp?d=528anda=3346 [Accessed February 2009].

National Autistic Society (2008) *SPELL. What is the SPELL Framework*? Available at: www.autism.org.uk/nas/jsp/polopoly.jsp?d=528anda=3362 [Accessed February 2009].

National Health Service National Services Scotland: Information Services Division. (NSS: ISD) Available at: www.isdscotland.org [Accessed February 2009].

National Initiative for Autism: Screening and Assessment (NIASA) (2003) National Autism Plan for Children (NAPC): *Plan for the identification, assessment, diagnosis and access to early interventions for pre-school and primary school aged children with autism spectrum disorders.* London: National Autistic Society.

Nind, M. (1999) Intensive interaction and autism: a useful approach? *British Journal of Special Education,* 26(2), 96-102.

Nordoff, P. and Robbins, C. (1977) *Creative Music Therapy.* New York: John Day Company.

Nordoff, P. and Robbins, C. (1998) *Creative Music Therapy,* (2nd Edition), St. Louis, MO: MMB Music Incorporated.

Olweus, D. (1992) Victimization of peers: antecedents and long-term outcomes. In: K.H. Rubin, and J.D. Asenddorf, (Eds.) *Social Withdrawal, Inhibition and Shyness in Childhood.* Hillsdale, NJ: Lawrence Erlbaum Associates.

Ozonoff, S., Rogers, S. and Hendren, R. (Eds.) (2003) *Autism Spectrum Disorders. A Research Review for Practitioners.* Virginia: American Psychiatric Publishing.

Peacock, G., Forrest, A. and Mills. R. (1996) *Autism: The Invisible Children*. London: National Autistic Society.

Peeters, T. (1997) *Autism: From theoretical understanding to educational intervention.* London Whurr Publishers.

Perepa, P. (2007) Are ASD services for minority ethnic communities accessible?, *Good Autism Practice,* 8, 2.

Plimley, L. and Bowen, M. (2006) *Supporting Pupils with Autistic Spectrum Disorders. A Guide for School Support Staff.* London: Paul Chapman.

Powers, M. D. (2000) *Children with Autism: A Parents' Guide.* Bethesda: Woodbine House Inc.

Public Health Institute of Scotland (2001) *Autistic Spectrum Disorders - Needs Assessment Report.* (The PHIS Report) Glasgow: PHIS/NHS Scotland. Available at: http://www.scottishautismnetwork.org.uk/phisreport1.pdf [Accessed February 2009].

Public Health Institute of Scotland (2003) *Needs Assessment Report on Child and Adolescent Mental Health: Final Report.* Glasgow: Public Health Institute of Scotland (PHIS). Available at: www.wellscotland.info/uploads/file.php?serve=1133631282-needs-assessment-report-2003.pdfandaction=download [Accessed February 2009].

Reading, J. (1999) Towards equity in service provision-commentary, *Tizard Learning Disability Review,* 4, 4, 6-15.

Reid, B. and Batten, A. (2006) *B is for bullied: the experiences of children with autism and their families*, London: National Autistic Society.

Rinaldi, W. (2008) *Social use of Language Programme* (SULP) Available at: www.wendyrinaldi.com [Accessed February 2009].

Robinson, A. (2005) *VIS-RAM: A Dynamic Assessment and Intervention for Adolescents and Adults with Asperger syndrome,* Centre for Education and Training in Autism, chapter 1: PhD in progress.

Robinson, A. (2006 and 2007) *VIS-RAM: A Dynamic Assessment and Intervention for Adolescents and Adults with Asperger syndrome,* Centre for Education and Training in Autism. PhD in progress.

Russell, E., Mataix Cols, D., Anson, M. and Murphy, D. (2005) Obsessions and compulsions in Asperger's Syndrome and high functioning autism, *British Journal of Psychiatry,* 186, 525-528.

Russell, E. and Sofronoff, K. (2004) Anxiety and social worries in children with Asperger's Syndrome, *Australian and New Zealand Journal of Psychiatry,* 39, 633-638.

Rutter, M., and Bartak, L. (1973) Special educational treatment of autistic children: a Comparative study, II Follow-up findings and Implications for services. *Journal of Child Psychology and Psychiatry,* 14, 241-270.

Salovey, P. and Mayer, J. D. (1990) Emotional intelligence, *Imagination, Cognition, and Personality,* 9, 185-211.

Schopler. E., Reichler. R.J., and Lansing, M. (1980) *Individualized assessment and treatment for autistic and developmentally disabled children, Vol. 2: Teaching strategies for parents and professional.* Austin, TX: Pro-Ed.

Schopler, E., Reichler, R. J., Bashford, A., Lansing, M. D. and Marcus, L. M. (1990) *Volume 1 Psycho educational Profile revised (PEP-R).* Texas: PRO-ED.

Schopler, E., Lansing, M.D., Reichler, R.J., and Marcus, L.M. (2005*) Psycho educational Profile-Third Edition. PEP-3.* Los Angeles: Western Psychological Services.

Schroeder, A. (1998) *Socially Speaking. Pragmatic Social Skills Programme for Pupils with Mild to Moderate Learning Disabilities.* Wisbech, Cambridgeshire: LDA Publishers.

Schuler AL. (2003) Beyond echoplaylia: promoting language in children with autism. *Autism,* 7(4):455-69.

Schwartz, I.S., Garfinkel, A.N. and Bauer, J. (1998) The Picture Exchange Communication System: Communicative outcomes for young children with disabilities. *Topics in Early Childhood Special Education,* 18, 144-159.

Scottish Executive (2003a) *Improving Health in Scotland: The Challenge.* Scottish Executive. Edinburgh: Scottish Executive. Available at:

http://www.scotland.gov.uk/Resource/Doc/47034/0013854.pdf [Accessed February 2009].

Scottish Executive (2003b) *An introduction to the Mental Health (Care and Treatment) (Scotland) Act*. Edinburgh: Scottish Executive. Available at: www.opsi.gov.uk/legislation/scotland/acts2003/asp_20030013_en_1 [Accessed February 2009].

Scottish Executive (2003c) *Mental Health Improvement: What works? A briefing for the Scottish Executive*. Available at: www.wellscotland.info/uploads/file.php?serve=1134577374-MHI-WhatWorks.pdfandaction=download [Accessed February 2009].

Scottish Executive (2003d) *National Programme for improving Mental Health and Well-being action plan 2003–2006* (September) Edinburgh: Scottish Executive. Available at: www.scotland.gov.uk/Publications/2003/09/18193/26506 [Accessed February 2009].

Scottish Executive (2004a) *Education (Additional Support for Learning) (Scotland) Act* Edinburgh: Scottish Executive. Available at: www.opsi.gov.uk/legislation/scotland/acts2004/asp_20040004_en_1 [Accessed February 2009].

Scottish Executive (2004b) *Changing Childhood report*. Available at: http://www.scotland.gov.uk/Publications/2006/04/24104745/0 [Accessed February 2009].

Scottish Executive Health Promoting Schools Unit (2004c) *Being Well - Doing Well: A Framework for Health Promoting Schools in Scotland.* Dundee: Scottish Executive Health Promoting Schools Unit. Available at: www.ltscotland.org.uk/Images/Beingwelldoingwell_tcm4-121991.pdf [Accessed February 2009].

Scottish Executive (2004d) *Mental Health, Mental Well-being and Mental Health Improvement: What do they mean? A practical guide to terms and definitions*. Edinburgh: Scottish Executive. Available at: www.wellscotland.info/information-resources.html#mentalhealth [Accessed February 2009].

Scottish Executive (2005a) *Health for All Children 4: Guidance on Implementation in Scotland.* Edinburgh. Scottish Executive. Available at: www.scotland.gov.uk/Publications/2005/04/15161325 [Accessed February 2009].

Scottish Executive (2005b) *The Mental Health of Children and Young People: A Framework for Promotion, Prevention and Care*. Edinburgh: Scottish Executive. Available at: www.scotland.gov.uk/Publications/2005/10/2191333/13337 [Accessed February 2009].

Scottish Executive (2005c) *Supporting Children's Learning (Code of Practice)* Edinburgh: Scottish Executive. Available at: www.scotland.gov.uk/Publications/2005/08/15105817 [Accessed February 2009].

Scottish Executive (2005d) *Allied Health Professionals (AHP): Child Health Services*. Available at: http://www.scotland.gov.uk/Publications/2005/09/06111820/18209 [Accessed February 2009].

Scottish Executive (2005e) *Getting it right for every child: proposals for Action: Section 3 Integrated Assessment, planning and Recording Framework. Supporting Paper 1: The process and content of an Integrated Framework and the implications for implementation*. Edinburgh: The Scottish Government. Available at: www.scotland.gov.uk/Publications/2005/07/25112327/23294. [Accessed February 2009].

Scottish Executive (2006a) *Assessment is for Learning*. Learning and Teaching Scotland. Available at: www.scotland.gov.uk/Publications/2006/09/15090146/1 [Accessed February 2009].

Scottish Executive (2006b). *Parents as Partners in Their Children's Learning: Toolkit.* Edinburgh: Scottish Executive. Available at: www.scotland.gov.uk/Publications/2006/09/07091311/0 [Accessed February 2009].

Scottish Executive (2006c) *Getting it Right for Every Child: Implementation Plan.* Edinburgh: Scottish Executive. Available at: www.scotland.gov.uk/Publications/2006/06/22092413/0 [Accessed February 2009].

Scottish Government (2006d) *Family Law (Scotland) Act.* Scottish Government. Edinburgh: The Scottish Government. Available at: www.opsi.gov.uk/legislation/scotland/acts2006/asp_20060002_en_1 [Accessed February 2009].

Scottish Government (2006e) *Scottish Schools (Parental Involvement) Act 2006*. Edinburgh: The Scottish Government. Available at: www.opsi.gov.uk/legislation/scotland/acts2006/pdf/asp_20060008_en.pdf [Accessed February 2009].

Scottish Government (2007a) *The Concordat*. Available at: http://www.scotland.gov.uk/Publications/2006/04/24104745/0 [Accessed February 2009].

Scottish Government (2007b) *Scottish Budget Spending Review, Chapter 8 – A National Performance Framework*. Available at: http://www.scotland.gov.uk/Publications/2007/11/13092240/9 [Accessed February 2009].

Scottish Government (2007c) *United Nations Convention on The Rights of the Child. A Report on Implementation of the UN Convention on The Rights of the Child in Scotland 1999-2007.* Edinburgh: Scottish Executive. Available at: www.scotland.gov.uk/Publications/2007/07/30114126/0 [Accessed February 2009].

Scottish Government (2007d) *Building Excellence: Exploring the Implications of the Curriculum for Excellence for School Buildings*. Edinburgh: The Scottish Government. Available at: http://www.scotland.gov.uk/Publications/2007/12/14115428/0 [Accessed February 2009].

Scottish Government (2007e) *Towards a mentally flourishing Scotland.* Available at: http://www.scotland.gov.uk/Resource/Doc/201215/0053753.pdf [Accessed February 2009].

Scottish Government (2008a) *Early Years Framework.* Edinburgh: The Scottish Government. Available at www.scotland.gov.uk/earlyyearsframework [Accessed February 2009].

Scottish Government (2008b) *A Curriculum for Excellence: Building the Curriculum 3: A Framework for Learning and Teaching.* Edinburgh: The Scottish Government. Available at:

www.scotland.gov.uk/Publications/2008/06/06104407/13 [Accessed February 2009].

Scottish Government (2008c) *Supporting Children's Learning (Code of Practice)* Edinburgh: Scottish Government. Available at:

www.scotland.gov.uk/Publications/2005/08/15105817 [Accessed February 2009].

Scottish Government (2008d) *Scottish Exchange of Educational Data (ScotXed)* Edinburgh: The Scottish Government. Available at: www.scotxed.net/jahia/Jahia [Accessed February 2009].

Scottish Intercollegiate Guidelines Network (SIGN) (2007) *Assessment, diagnosis and clinical interventions for children and young people with autism spectrum disorders* (SIGN publication 98) Available at: www.sign.ac.uk/guidelines/published/numlist.html [Accessed February 2009].

Scottish Needs Assessment Programme (SNAP) (2000) *Mental Health Promotion Among Young People*. Glasgow: SNAP.

Scottish Office (1999) *Towards a Healthier Scotland. A White Paper on Health*. The Stationery Office. Available at: www.scotland.gov.uk/library/documents-w7/tahs-00.htm [Accessed February 2009].

Scottish Parliament (2000) *The Standards in Scotland's Schools etc Act (2000)* Available at:

www.hmso.gov.uk/legislation/scotland/acts2000/20000006.htm [Accessed February 2009].

Scottish Society for Autism (2007, 2008*) SSA, Advisory cases* – Reported by Anna Robinson, author.

Shah, R. (1995) *The silent minority: children with disabilities in Asian families*. 2nd Edition. London: National Children's Bureau.

Shea, Victoria (2004) A perspective on the research literature related to early intensive behavioral intervention (Lovaas) for young children with autism, *Autism*, 8(4) 349-36.

Shields, J. (2001) The NAS EarlyBird programme. Partnership with Parents in Early Intervention. *Autism*, 5 (1) 49-56. Available at: http://aut.sagepub.com/cgi/content/abstract/5/1/49?ck=nck [Accessed February 2009].

Sigman, M., Spence S.J. and Ting Wang, A. (2006) Autism from Developmental and Neuropsychological Perspectives, *Annual Review of Clinical Psychology,* 2, 327-355.
Silver M, Oakes P. (2001*)* Evaluation of a new computer intervention to teach people with autism or Asperger syndrome to recognize and predict emotions in others. *Autism,* 5(3): 299-316.

Smith Myles, B. and Andreon. D. (2001) *Asperger Syndrome and Adolescence: Practical Solutions for School Success.* Kansas: Autism Asperger Publishing Company.

Smith Myles, B. and Simpson, R. (2001) Understanding the Hidden Curriculum: An essential social skill for children and youth with Asperger's syndrome, *Intervention in School and Clinic,* 36, 5, 279-286.

Sofronoff, K., and Attwood, T. (2003) A cognitive behaviour therapy intervention for anxiety in children with Asperger syndrome. *Good Autism Practice*, 6, 1-8.

Stakes, R. and Hornby, G. (2000) *Meeting Special Needs in Mainstream Schools*. London. David Fulton.

Stewart, M.E., Barnard, L., Pearson, J., Hasan, R. and O'Brien, G. (2006) Presentation of depression in autism and Asperger Syndrome – A review, *Autism,* 10, 1, 103-116.

Stoddart, K. P. (2004) *Children, Youth and Adults with Asperger Syndrome: Integrating Multiple Perspectives.* London: Jessica Kingsley.

Sussman, F. (1999) *More Than Words: Helping Parents Promote Communication and Social Skills in Children with Autistic Spectrum Disorders.* Oxford: Winslow Press.

Sutton, P.W., Love, J.G., Bell, J., Christie, E., Mayrhofer, A., Millman, Y., Williams, H. and Yuill, C. (2005) *The Emotional Well-Being of Young People: A Review of the Literature.* School of Applied Social Studies. Aberdeen: Robert Gordon University.

Symon, J. (2001) Parent Education for Autism: Issues in Providing Services at a Distance, *Journal of Positive Behaviour Interventions,* 3, 3.

Tait, C. and Dunlop, A.W. (2005) *The Impact of Training on Practice: Insights from postgraduate study of autism.* Inclusion in Special Education Conference.

Tantum, D. (1988) Asperger's syndrome, *Journal of Psychology and Psychiatry,* 29, 245-253.

Tantum, D. (2000) Psychological disorder in adolescents and adults with Asperger syndrome, *Autism*, 4, 1, 47-62.

Trevarthen, C. (2000) Autism as a neurodevelopmental disorder affecting communication and learning in early childhood: Prenatal origins, post natal course and effective educational support, *Prostoglandins, Leucotrines and Essential Fatty Acids,* Vol. 63 (1/2), 41- 46.

Trevarthen, C., Aitken, K., Papoudi, D. and Robarts, J. (1998) *Children with autism.* 2nd Edition. London: Jessica Kingsley.

Trevarthen, C. and Aitken, K. (2001) Intersubjective foundations in human psychological development. Annual Research Review, *The Journal of Child Psychology and Psychiatry and Allied Disciplines.*42, 3-48.

Vermeulen, P. (2001) *Autistic Thinking: This is the Title.* London: Jessica Kingsley.

Vygotsky, L. S. (1978) *Mind in Society: The Development of Higher Mental Processes.* Cambridge, MA: Harvard University Press.

Watson, J. and Fisher, A. (1997) Evaluation the effectiveness of Intensive Interaction teaching with pupils with profound and complex learning difficulties. *British Journal of Special Education,* 24(2), 80-87.

Weare, K. (2004) *Developing the Emotionally Literate School.* London: Paul Chapman.

White, A. (2004) Cognitive behavioural therapy in children with autistic spectrum disorder. In Bazian Ltd (Ed) *STEER: Succinct and Timely Evaluated Evidence Reviews,* 4(5) Southampton: Bazian Ltd and Wessex Institute for Health Research and Development, University of Southampton.

Whitely, P. and Shattock, P. (2002) Biochemical aspects in autism spectrum disorders: updating the opioid-excess theory and presenting new opportunities for biomedical intervention. *Expert Opinion on Therapeutic Targets,* 6(2), 175-183.

Williams, C. and Wright, B. (2004) *How to Live with Autism and Asperger Syndrome.* London: Jessica Kingsley.

Williams, D. (1996) *Autism: An Inside Out Approach*, London: Jessica Kingsley.

Williams, K.R. and Wishart, G. (2003) The Son-Rise Program intervention for autism: an investigation into family experiences. *Journal of Intellectual Disability Research*, 47, 4/5, 291-299.

Wing, L. (1981) Asperger's Syndrome: a clinical account, *Psychological Medicine,* 11,115-130.

Wing, L. (1996) *The Autistic Spectrum*. London: Constable.

Wing, L. and Gould, J. (1979) Severe impairments of social interaction and associated abnormalities in children: epidemiology and classification, *Journal of Autism and Developmental Disorders,* 9, 11-29.

Wolfberg, P.J. and Schuler, A.L. (1993) Integrated play groups: a model for promoting the social and cognitive dimensions of play in children with autism. *Journal of Autism and Developmental Disorders,* 23(3): 467-89.

World Health Organization (1992) *International Classification of Diseases: Tenth Revision*. Geneva: World Health Organisation.

Yang, T.R., Wolfberg, P.J., Wu, S.C. and Hwu, P.Y. (2003) Supporting children on the autism spectrum in peer play at home and school: piloting the integrated playgroups model in Taiwan. *Autism,* 7(4):437-53.

Zercher, C., Hunt, P., Schuler, A. and Webster, J. (2001) Increasing Joint Attention, Play and Language through Peer Supported Play. *Autism,* 5 (4): 374-98.